HARDPRESS.NET
HOME OF HARD-TO-FIND BOOKS

The Productions, Industry, and Resources of New South Wales
by Charles St. Julian

Address:
HardPress
8345 NW 66TH ST #2561
MIAMI FL 33166-2626
USA
Email: info@hardpress.net

THE

PRODUCTIONS, INDUSTRY, AND RESOURCES

OF

NEW SOUTH WALES.

BY

CHARLES ST. JULIAN, AND EDWARD K. SILVESTER.

SYDNEY:

J. MOORE, GEORGE-STREET.

1853.

SYDNEY:
PRINTED BY KEMP AND FAIRFAX,
LOWER GEORGE STREET.

CARPENTER

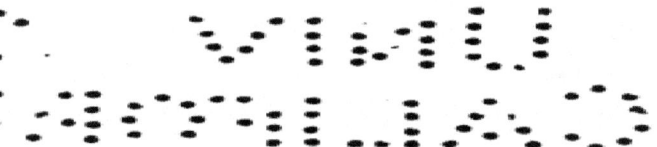

ADVERTISEMENT.

THE following work is a mere reprint of a series of papers which have appeared from time to time in the *Sydney Morning Herald*.

Many of them were written and published so long as two years back, but the severe and protracted illness of one of the authors, and other causes, with which it is unnecessary to trouble the reader, produced delay.

Much improvement might doubtless be effected by a revision of these papers. From the mode in which they have been printed, however, such a revision would, at the present time, be very difficult, if not totally impracticable.

CONTENTS.

INTRODUCTION.

As recent events will cause the regards of the whole civilized world to be fixed upon this colony as a field for enterprise, it is absolutely necessary that accurate information relative to the extent and nature of that field should be provided. It is equally necessary that this information should be given in a plain and practical shape. Our desire, therefore, has been to produce such a work as may be read and understood by all. The use of scientific terms and phrases, with which the ordinary reader is not likely to be acquainted, has consequently been, as much as possible, avoided.

On the face of every nation Nature has stamped the features wherein intelligence and experience may read the charecter and resources which it possesses.

Its climate, soil, position, and natural productions form the index which points out to civilized man the direction in which to turn his energies and his enterprise, and to ascertain

B 2

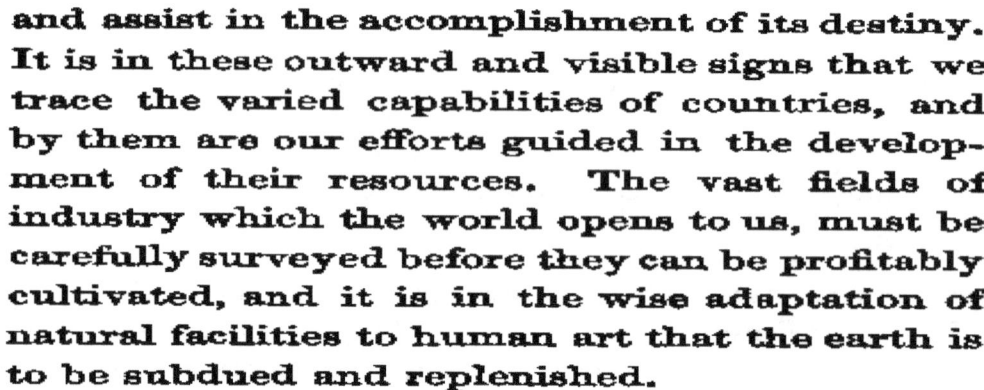

and assist in the accomplishment of its destiny. It is in these outward and visible signs that we trace the varied capabilities of countries, and by them are our efforts guided in the development of their resources. The vast fields of industry which the world opens to us, must be carefully surveyed before they can be profitably cultivated, and it is in the wise adaptation of natural facilities to human art that the earth is to be subdued and replenished.

Every continent, every zone, every country has its own peculiar fitness for the industrial pursuits of man ; and it is by careful examination of this fitness that we educate, as it were, the various districts of the world, and train up nations in the way they should go.

In these times, indeed, when the earth is grown grey with the experience of thousands of years ; when science has subdued the elements, and industry turns to the use of man every production which can be derived from it ; it is the more necessary that we should consider well what position in the world we are to assume—it is right that we should count our resources and weigh our natural treasures, and ponder carefully how we may turn them to the best account.

We find under what seems to be a special

ordination of Providence, that in this, as in other quarters of the globe, the wild aboriginal inhabitants give way before the civilized races of the world ; it would seem indeed, that the European races are ultimately to be spread all over the earth — that under the light of science, every continent however varying in climate and soil, is to be, at least to a very large extent, peopled by these races. And we find too, with slight modifications, the wants of these races, wherever they may accidentally be placed, assimilate. The same food, the same clothing, the same appliances of usefulness, comfort, and luxury are required wherever we find civilized Europeans settled. The same vessels traverse the waves of the Atlantic and Pacific, the Northern and the Southern Oceans ; the same vehicles, the same principles of conveyance, obtain in Europe as do in America ; in all the continents the same animals are reared for the purposes of food and for service in the domestic arts ; and the products of the soil, various as they are, become the common property of all.

Whatever then may be the peculiarities of production existent in any particular region, that production must in its adaptation to the purposes of civilization be convertible by some industrial process into something useful, not only to the inhabitants of the spot where it is produced, but to civilized man every where. This is the principle on which all commerce is based; this is the principle on which labour, the punishment and the portion of the human family, is made subservient to the great design of peopling the world and filling it with enlightenment. It is on this principle that we are entitled to believe that in the fulness of time all the families of the world will be united together, because each will be the producer of something which custom or exigency renders indispensable to the rest. Thus there must be great grain producing nations, such as Egypt, South America, and the European nations round the Baltic; there must be countries growing animal food for man from the richness of their natural grasses, such as Ireland and Australia; there must be wool growing countries, and cotton growing countries; lands where wine and oil, the fig, the olive, and the pomegranate flourish, and the more sterile wastes where the treasures for man's use lie hidden beneath the surface till brought to light by human art. The cedar and the oak, the mahogany and the satin-wood, are all alike required in other countries than those where each is produced; and it not unfrequently happens, that the skill and ingenuity of one country invests the productions of another with nearly all their value.

A grand and sublime system of the division of labour seems to prevail over the earth, and to each clime, to each hemisphere — is appropriated its allotted share. Growing with the growth of the world, human labour has advanced step by step, until it has itself half obliterated the curse by which it was entailed on mankind.

In its creative powers, its wonderful processes, its elevating and intellectual tendencies, it has redeemed mankind from the low barbarism to which in our earlier condition we were condemned. The beauties and the wonders of creation become ennobled by the discoveries of art and science, and the mind is exalted, the passions chastened and subdued, the wisdom strengthened and enlarged in the lofty appreciation which we are now enabled to give to the wondrous design of the universe.

Nor can we when we look around and see the spread of industrial science—the desire that exists, not only to furnish necessaries and comforts for our support and sustenance, but to delight the senses and to conquer what seemed impassable obstacles to human improvement, human happiness, and human fellowship – regard this magnificent development of the connexion of the skill of man with the productions of the earth, otherwise than as the great moral and social amelioration of our condition. Industrial pursuits as they are now prosecuted are, we take it, almost apostolic in their influences upon the world. It is to these that we must trace the peopling of the earth in its lonely and desolate places. It is to these that we must ascribe the spirit of civilization which is spreading over the world, that is gradually dispelling heathen barbarism and heathen crime, and preparing the advent of a holy and universal fellowship.

It is in no profane spirit, with no light and unseemly regard to those higher institutions of morality and religion which we have been taught to reverence and have learned to love, that we say we regard industrial science as the great missionary engine of civilization. While one island of the world remains unexplored there is no limit to its energies — while one acre of the giant field for its enterprise remains uncultivated there is no pause in its exertions. There is no obstacle, no difficulty which it cannot surmount, for obstacles and difficulties are only suggestive of fresh designs on which it may employ itself.

The ocean rolls in vain across its path; it becomes the passive agent of enterprise; the river and the mountain are subdued, the desert is reclaimed, the morass made fertile, the dull ore becomes impregnate with life and beauty, and the solid rock and giant tree glow with unknown majesty and splendour.

Silently but surely this spirit of industry is taking possession of the world; silently but surely it is setting down countless multitudes in remote solitudes, and investing them with all the comforts, all the intellectual advancement of modern civilization. It is associating communities one with another, by establishing a system of mutual dependence, by an interchange of the labours of one nation for the benefit of another.

And while thus fulfilling one revelation of Scripture, that the earth shall bring forth its fruit with increase—this great civilizer of the universe is the promoter of the fulfilment of another. It is impossible that the artizan can see the works of his hands, can see the marvellous ingenuity, the bold and triumphant design which these works display, without having his intellect exercised and strengthened. To him the works of the Great Creator must

assume a higher and more ennobling teaching
than that which they impart in their wild solitudes. He sees in every thing that comes under
his hand the unmistakeable evidence of wise
and benevolent design. He finds that there is
nothing that God has made which is not very
good ; nothing that the plastic hand of
Nature has formed that man, in the
heritage of labour to which he is doomed,
cannot turn to his own advantage. He will
learn too, that there is some consolation in this
heritage of labour in the belief that it is giving
him the light of a high and holy knowledge ;
that it is teaching him to perform his part in
the world's regeneration, and to look upon
man as his brother wherever he may find him ;
that it is imparting kindly charities and
soft amenities to the human race ; that it is
breaking down prejudices and clearing away
animosities ; that it is teaching all men to
appreciate more fully the blessings they enjoy,
and to look up in thankfulness to that great
and benevolent Being who has provided them ;
that while it is peopling the solitude and
making glad the desert with the sounds and
sights of busy life, it will preach as it goes
along its path to hearts exalted and refined,
the divinity of the Almighty Creator, the duty

of man to his Lord and to his neighbour, "till the earth shall be filled with the knowledge of God as the waters cover the sea."

PART I.

Aboriginal Inhabitants—Wild Animals—Indigenous Vegetable Productions—Bush-craft.

———

THERE are few countries in the world which afford so wide a field for the researches of the naturalist as New South Wales. His list of quadrupeds may soon, indeed, be completed, but in pursuing the other branches of his science he will find an ample compensation for this deficiency. Our feathered tribes and the denizens of our waters are exceedingly numerous and varied in species. Of the inferior animals the varieties are so great, that, notwithstanding the attention and labour which many gentlemen of the highest scientific attainments have devoted to this species of research, new specimens are frequently being discovered. To the botanist and the geologist the field of research may be almost described as inexhaustible.

THE ABORIGINES—THEIR ARTS OF LIFE.

The aboriginal tribes of this territory stand lower in the scale of humanity than, perhaps, any other race of men upon earth; and in their association with the white man they have unhappily shown far greater aptitude in picking up his vices than in acquiring such useful information as an attentive observation of his proceedings would serve to impart. As might be expected, these people have never availed themselves, to any great extent, of the natural wealth by which they are surrounded, neither has the teaching and example of their Anglo-Saxon brethren been able to open their eyes to the advantages of civilization. In those arts of forest and prairie life, which may almost be considered as the result of mere animal instinct rather than of human reason, they are, nevertheless, but little inferior to other savages. Much useful information was acquired by our pioneer colonists from these untaught denizens of the wild; and still, we doubt not, many valuable hints might be received by an attentive observation of their habits and proceedings. With cultivation even of the most rude nature they were originally unacquainted; and even at the present time, when they see around them so many agriculturists, from an observance of whose motions they might acquire all the knowledge which is necessary, they prefer a dependence upon the spontaneous productions of nature to the labor of subduing the earth, and drawing from a particular spot their supplies of vegetable food. They are, in fact, excellent practical botanists. An aboriginal Australian will find an abundance of food where most white men would perish from hunger. It is in reference to this knowledge, which tradition, experience, and necessity has taught them, of the natural productions of the regions over which they wander, and to their general skill and acuteness in what may be termed bush-craft, that the settlers may with most profit submit to their instruction.

The wild animals of Australia are nearly all caught or killed in one way or another by the blacks; many of them being used for food, which the civilised races have never applied to such a purpose. From the skins of opossums, they make very excellent and hand-some winter cloaks, which were the only articles properly describable as clothing among them, until the importation of the favorite blanket. Girdles and small nets they manu-facture from vegetable fibres. Their canoes are of the simplest structure, being formed of a mere sheet of bark joined at the ends : in some parts of the continent they are contented with the still more primitive conveyance of a small raft. Vessels for carrying water are con-structed of bark or wood. Their weapons both for war and the chase, are made with considerable skill, although these weapons are of the simplest kind—spears, clubs of various forms, and shields ; archery is unknown to them, but their want of this knowledge is made up by the great skill and force with which they throw their spears and boomerangs. Their vegetable food is exceedingly varied, and they exhibit much skill in destroying the deleterious properties which some of the wild fruits and roots possess, so as to render them fit for food.

Their knowledge of the mineral kingdom and their application of its products, extend only to the use of the pigments with which they color their bodies at times of festivity, and to the use of flint for pointing their weapons.

Their dwellings, when they construct any, are of the simplest kind, usually a mere arch of boughs, affording some slight shelter to the upper part of the body, while the lower limbs are stretched out towards the fire which burns at a short distance ; for rough weather a similarly shaped structure of bark is put up, but some of the central and northern tribes erect more substantial huts in a bee-hive form, about four feet high, and six or eight feet in diameter. These are made of boughs or thatch roughly plastered over, and entered by a hole just large enough for a man to crawl through. On the northern coasts two storied huts have been found ; saplings are driven into the ground with their forked ends uppermost ; upon these thin poles are laid, and upon the frame thus constructed a bark floor is placed, arched over by a shallow bark roof : this mode of building is resorted to in order to avoid lying on the damp ground during wet seasons.

QUADRUPEDS.

The first of the Australian quadrupeds, and the largest existing animal of the marsupial family, to which the gigantic Diprotodon belonged,* is the KANGAROO ; as a class of animals the kangaroos are now so well known, not only by the description of explorers and naturalists, but by the transmission of specimens to all parts of Europe, that it is unnecessary to describe their appearance. There are a great many varieties of this animal, but the variation is not so much in appearance as in size and in their places of resort. The forester is the largest of the family, and is frequently found of two hundred pounds weight. The large males of this species are generally called the " old man kangaroo" by the colonists, and by such of the aborigines as have a smattering of English ; an accomplishment, by-the-by, which few of them are without. The wallaby and the pademelon are much smaller, the former inhabiting rocky grounds, and the latter being found exclusively in what is termed brush lands. The average weight of the wallaby is about 12 or 14 pounds, and that of the pademelon about nine or ten pounds. The kangaroo rat seldom weighs more than three or four pounds, and is found in various localities, even in the most barren scrub. It is not, as its name would import, anything of the rat species; but a perfect kangaroo in miniature.

* Most of the bones of one of these animals are now in the Australian Museum, and we believe that the Curator intends to erect a skeleton. The living animal must have been from fourteen to sixteen feet in height. It was a sort of kola, or native bear. There is also in the Museum the under jaw of a *true kangaroo*, which must have been upwards of twenty feet high.

D

The rock wallaby is found in large numbers on many of the small islands near the coast, as well as the main land. Of all these kinds there are several varieties. One species, commonly called the Kangaroo Mouse, discovered by Sir Thomas Mitchell, is not larger than the common field mouse.

What the colonists term "brush" lands are those covered with tall trees growing so near each other and being so closely matted together by underwood, parasites, and creepers, as to be wholly impassable. "Scrub" is a denomination applied to a more stunted but equally tangled kind of vegetation, composed of dwarf trees, bushes, and creeping or other plants. This kind of land, however, is more easily traversed than the brush ; first, because the growth is seldom so strong but that a passage may be forced through it in most places ; and, secondly, because open spaces and tracks are more frequently met with.

The larger Kangaroos, which inhabit the open forest lands and the plains, are usually taken by coursing ; a kind of sport in which, owing to the nature of the country and of the animal pursued, the horses, dogs, and huntsmen have generally their work to do. The kangaroo bounds off at a pace which requires his pursuers to use their best speed in following him, and the great height to which he can spring enables him to clear all ordinary impediments to his progress.

For the most part, therefore, his course is straightforward, through thick and thin, and in anything of a difficult country, more especially in some of the mountain regions, none but a good steed and a good rider can follow with any chance of success. The stock-horses bred in the colony are admirably adapted to this kind of service. Kangaroo hounds are also bred and trained in the colony by the lovers of this sport, and a good deal of training, indeed, is necessary, for the kangaroo, besides the speed and peculiarity of his course, is a much more formidable antagonist to the canine race, and even to their biped masters, than would at first sight appear. The fore feet of this animal are very short, and are not used by him for the purposes of ordinary locomotion, but in cropping the herbage on which he feeds—in fact, as hands. The hinder legs, however, are large and powerful, and are armed with sharp hooked claws of great size and strength, with which he speedily disembowels any unfortunate dog who approaches him incautiously when he is standing at bay; when hard pressed a kangaroo will stand with his back to a tree, and a dog venturing to attack him in this position is apt to be caught by the assaulted animal with one of his forepaws and held to the breast, while with a single stroke of the hind foot he is either destroyed or seriously injured. A man approaching the animal in front would stand a great chance of being similarly treated. On these occasions the huntsmen usually get behind the kangaroo and cleave his skull, or fire a charge into him from a short distance. A dog seldom attacks the kangaroo when thus standing at bay without receiving a severe hurt for his pains ; but if the sportsman can manage to lay hold of the animal's massive tail and keep it off the ground, the dogs will speedily kill him, for, in that case, he is unable to raise either of the formidable hind feet, and his canine assailants may spring at his throat with impunity. Occasionally the pursued "old man" will make for a waterhole, and placing himself in a shallow, will drown any dog which approaches him ; in this case the only resource is a shot. A well-trained dog will spring at a kangaroo while he is bounding, and seizing him by the root of the tail will bring him forcibly to the ground—suddenly quitting his hold, the dog will then seize the kangaroo by the throat, and by a vigorous shaking put a stop to all further resistance on his part. Young dogs, however, in attempting this manœuvre are frequently hurt, and sometimes killed by a rending blow from one of the hind feet.

The pademelon is sought for by the sportsman, either alone or aided by a good dog, and is brought down with the gun. A good deal of experience in bush-craft, however, is necessary for the acquisition of sufficient skill and quickness in this kind of shooting, owing to the rapidity with which the animal, on being alarmed, bounds away through the underwood, to the concealment which the underwood affords him, and to the irregularity of his course. Old bushmen, nevertheless, are very successful in this sport, when they think fit to pursue it, and the blacks are peculiarly skilful in capturing and killing the pademelon after their own fashion. This species of the kangaroo seems to have a taste for music; for if the sportsman approaches him cautiously whistling without intermission, in a low monotonous tone as he advances, the amused animal will allow him to go sufficiently near for a fair shot. When first started, the pademelon seldom goes far, and his bounds may be distinctly heard by the sportsman. The latter, therefore, if he has failed to get a shot at the fugitive, should remain stationary until the noise of the jumping has ceased; marking the direction in which the animal has gone, and approaching it cautiously, in the manner already mentioned, with a keen glance around him to detect the listening pademelon. He will by these means be very likely to succeed in securing his game.

The kangaroo-rat is less sought for than its larger relatives, except by the sawyers and splitters, to whom these animals yield many a fresh meal during their sojourn amidst the heavily timbered flats and ranges. They are very numerous, but are seldom seen in the day time. At night, however, with the exercise of due caution they are easily shot. The plan which is found most successful is the following. Strew ashes or white sand over a small space of ground, so as to form a light coloured spot upon which the dusky forms of the kangaroo rats may stand out in relief, amidst the surrounding darkness. At some distance—as far as possible, consistent with a clear discernment of the animals, and with the certainty of the shot,—the sportsman must crouch down, having his gun pointed towards the white spot, and resting upon a log or a forked stick. A little maize or some broken bread strewed over this white spot will attract the animals to it, and the hidden sportsman can hardly fail to secure one or more at a single shot. His movements, however, must be very slow and silent, and if he is concealed by a bush or a fallen tree, so much the better, for these little animals are very wary.

The flesh of all the kangaroos is good. The fore quarters, indeed, of the larger animals are somewhat inferior, and are usually given to the dogs ; but from the hinder quarters some fine steaks may be cut. These, cooked in the same manner as venison collops, are, to most palates, very little inferior to the latter. The flesh of the large kangaroo as well as that of the wallaby is often dressed in the shape of a hash, and in this form, also, it is excellent. But the most admired part of the kangaroo is his tail. This is of enormous size in proportion to the rest of the body, the tail of a full-grown forester usually weighing ten or twelve pounds. It makes a superb soup, very much superior to ox-tail. The wallaby too is most commonly used for soup. The pade-melon when cooked like a hare affords a dish with which the most fastidious gourmand might be satisfied. The flesh of the kangaroo-rat resembles that of a rabbit, and it eats best when cooked in the same manner. The last mentioned animal is but little eaten, except by thorough bushmen, owing to the prejudice excited by the unfortunate name which has been bestowed upon it, but those who have once conquered this prejudice usually become fond of it.

The OPOSSUMS, of which there are several varieties, are also marsupial animal, and are very numerous in the open forest and brush lands, their habitation is the hollows of large tress, from which they rarely venture out except at night. Shooting opossums is a very favorite sport for moonlight nights, when a great many may be killed by one whose eye is quick at detecting them, and whose skill as a marksman is sufficiently good to bring them from their elevated perches ; to a person who is well accustomed to its use, a long barrelled pistol is better for this purpose than a gun, first, because it is a more portable article in scrambling through the brushwood, and secondly, because it is frequently necessary to fire at a point immediately above the head of the sportsman. The presence of opossums may be detected by a peculiar shrill cry to which they give utterance ; or by the marks made by their claws in ascending the trees.

The opossum seldom weighs more than five or six pounds. Its flesh is good, but is not much used by the settlers ; it affords to the blacks, however, the largest portion of their animal food, as they are able to get the opossum with comparative ease, by climbing the tree on which it abides. A good dog will scent an opossum most readily ; the more readily indeed, because he generally gets the carcass of the little animal as his share of the spoil, the sportsman contenting himself with the skin. When the bushman's dog points out the locale of an opossum, the dog's master will often amuse himself by storming the dwelling of the concealed animal and capturing him at once. If he is in the hollow of a limb, the limb is cut off, and he is speedily turned out ; if he is in the body of a hollow tree the interior of which is accessible near the root, a fire is lit below, and the poor opossum is compelled either to come out and face his enemies or to be suffocated—he chooses the former alternative and is shot.

THE FLYING SQUIRREL is, likewise, a marsupial. There are several varieties of this animal, the largest of them being a little bigger than the opossum, and the smallest no larger than a common mouse. The peculiarity of these beautiful little animals is that their fore and hind legs have a membraneous connexion, covered with fur like the rest of the body, by means of which they are able to spring a considerable distance from tree to tree. The flying squirrel is shot only for its skin.

Most, if not all of the before mentioned animals are easily tamed; it is now no uncommon thing to see one or two of the smaller kangaroos quietly browsing on the grassy lawn near a colonist's dwelling; and an opossum is a frequent pet. The latter is a merry little fellow but rather mischievous; his gambols, however, are very frequently confined within the limits of a cage.

It is a matter of surprise that the kangaroos are not still more frequently domesticated. There are few animals more beautiful in aspect or more gentle in disposition. In the parks and grounds of our Australian gentry their presence would be peculiarly graceful and appropriate, and, as has already been demonstrated, they are useful as well as ornamental.

All these animals disappear rapidly as colonization advances, but many of the kangaroos, and especially the smaller kinds, are still numerous enough within a comparatively short distance of Sydney. In fact, there are few parts of the country more wild than some portions of the county of Cumberland within an easy day's journey of the metropolis. Most of the country between Sydney and the Lower

Hawkesbury is of this description. In the more distant wilds, where the colonists have not yet penetrated, or which they traverse but seldom, game of every description is still abundant.

The NATIVE DOG or DINGO* is very like an English fox in its aspect and general color. Some, however, are found of different colors. Its size, too, is much greater than that of the fox. It is generally about two feet high, and from two to three feet in length ; its jaws are powerful, its teeth large and strong, and the effects of its snapping bite are very severe. Two or three of these animals, therefore, (and they often hunt in small packs) would be a formidable enemy to man, if they were only courageous enough to attack him ; but happily the dingo has no such courage. He will not even attack the larger kinds of domestic animals. To poultry, sheep, and even to young calves, he is however, a most deadly foe, and the more so because of his malice ; for not content with the satisfaction of his hunger, he wantonly destroys or injures all within his reach. Vast numbers of sheep, some say hundreds of thousands, are annually destroyed by this pest.

For this reason, he is hunted out and destroyed without mercy by the graziers and

* The Dingo, although common enough in all parts of the territory to be classed among its indigenous animals, is believed to have been originally of foreign origin.

settlers, who are not content with the slow process of extirpating these enemies by the aid of dog and gun, but call strychnine to their aid ; deluding the dingo with a poisoned bait as housekeepers and warehousemen serve the rats. In some parts thay have been killed off very rapidly in this way, but they are still very numerous, even in the neighbourhood of Sydney.

When hunted like a fox with a pack of hounds, the dingo affords excellent sport. Formerly there were several regularly organized hunts in different parts of the country, but the famous period of monetary depression broke them up. Since the arrival of the present Governor, however, this sport has been revived, so far as the neighbourhood of the metropolis is concerned. Mr. George Fitz Roy, his Excellency's son and Private Secretary, has an excellent pack, and the old fox-hunter possessing sufficient influence to take his place among the sportsmen who attend the meetings of "the Fitz Roy hounds," may at the antipodes have as keen and exciting a struggle for "the brush" as in England. In most cases he may safely calculate upon a difficult country, and upon ample room for displaying his skill as a horseman, and for trying the metal of his nag. In the interior the dingo is hunted down with two or three dogs, or perhaps with a single hound, for any dog of ordinary size and power is more than a match for him. Sometimes he is shot, but

his tenacity of life is so extraordinary, that
with a wound, and sometimes with several
wounds, that would appear sufficient to cause
immediate death, he will make off.

The dingo is unable to bark, but howls fearfully; and in places where these animals are
numerous, they keep up a serenade which seldom fails to deprive a new colonist of his rest.

They do not bite with a steady hold after
the fashion of a dog, but their sharp angry
snap inflicts a severe wound. They are often
domesticated, but their orginal predilections
are never thoroughly subdued. No amount of
good feeding will preserve their honesty or
render them less spiteful in the vicinity of
a poultry yard or a sheep pen. They readily
breed, however, with the dogs of the graziers
and settlers, and the progeny is much esteemed.

The flesh of this animal is eaten by the
blacks, but the colonists, as might naturally
be supposed, never touch it. The skin of the
dingo has not hitherto been made any use of,
but the brushy and fox-like tail, and sometimes the head, is cut off by sportsmen as
a trophy.

The KOLA, so called by the aborigines, but
more commonly known among the settlers as
the native bear or monkey, is found in brush and
forest lands—chiefly in mountainous regions.
It is believed to feed principally upon leaves,
and climbs trees, after the manner of a bear, in
search of its food. In its slow movements and
its apparent indifference to surrounding objects

it is more like a sloth than a bear. Its ordinary size is about two feet in length by about a foot in height when standing upon its four legs, (which is not often the case,) the circumference of the body being about a foot and a-half. The fur of this animal is of a fine woolly texture, and principally of a dull grey color. The kola has no tail, — the absence of this appendage, its naked muzzle, and its bushy ears, give to the animal a singular aspect, in fact its appearance is a sort of caricature upon gentlemen of the legal profession with their wigs on. It is said to be good eating, but is not frequently met with, although believed to be numerous enough in some of the heavy brush lands of the wilderness which the colonists do not traverse. When seen, however, it may be easily captured, and the captor has no wildness of disposition to conquer, for the kola seems to all appearance perfectly contented in every situation. It has nevertheless been found difficult to rear this animal, owing principally it is believed, to a want of accurate knowledge as to the kind of herbage upon which it feeds and its mode of varying its diet.

The WOMBAT, sometimes called the native pig, is a burrowing animal, feeding chiefly upon roots. It is stout and heavy-bodied, and is generally about three feet in length. Its fur is very coarse and its skin tough. Its flesh, although red and coarse in appearance, resembles that of a pig in flavor, and is usually cooked by the colonists as they would cook fresh pork.

E

In some places the wombats are very numerous, and as they burrow near the surface, the blacks easily find the course of their underground passage by striking the earth and listening to the sound. By this means they trace out the animal, which they forthwith unearth and knock on the head. The burrow oftens runs to a very considerable distance, and it is dangerous to ride over land beneath which the wombat has labored, for the horse is very apt to break through, damaging his own shins and giving his rider a summerset. The wombat is easily taken alive and domesticated. Remains of wombats more than thrice the size of any now existing have been found in the Bathurst caves.

The PORCUPINE ANT-EATER is similar in its size and general appearance to the English hedge-hog, except that it has a long and slender snout, and has the power of protruding its tongue to a considerable distance. It is a burrowing animal, and although ordinarily of dull and slothful habits it makes its way into the ground with extraordinary rapidity ; in fact, considering its size, its muscular power is very great. The upper surface of the body is covered with thick spines of a dirty yellowish color, blackish at the points, and averaging about an inch and three quarters in length. Below these the body is covered with dark fur. When attacked or alarmed the animal will coil himself like a hedge-hog, and burying his nose in the earth, leave nothing but a round of prickles exposed, which neither man nor beast can touch with impunity. These animals, of which there are two species, are not very numerous, but may frequently be met with even in the vicinity of Sydney by those acquainted with their habits and with the mode of tracking them. The flesh is delicate, resembling that of a young sucking pig.

The NATIVE CAT is a very beautiful little animal, the larger species being about a foot long, and the smaller about the size of a common rat. The skin of the larger and best known kind is elegantly spotted, and the fur long and fine. Some have light colored spots upon a dark ground, and others dark spots upon a light ground ; but these variations are only accidental, and not, as some have imagined, the characteristics of a different species or sex. The fur of the smaller kind is grey and greyish white, beautifully mingled and pencilled, with black tips. The native cat is a carnivorous animal, but has to content itself with small prey. Occasionally it is troublesome among the hen roosts, but is easily captured. When the new military barracks in the vicinity of Sydney were in course of erection, the scanty remains of the workmen's food, which lay about, attracted great numbers of these animals, who came either to feed upon the fragments, or upon the rats which these fragments attracted. They are pretty numerous in most parts of the colony, and may be readily hunted out with the aid of a dog, or taken in traps. They are seldom used for food, even by the blacks. They are easily tamed. There are other varieties of this animal no larger than a common mouse.

The BANDICOOT is a short-legged animal, from twelve to sixteen inches in length, with a coarse skin of a pale brown color, and a long and pointed snout. Bandicoots are very numerous, even in the neighbourhood of the metropolis, and, feeding chiefly on roots, are found very destructive in some of the gardens. They are particularly shy and wary, and are consequently not to be taken by the sportsman without the exercise of some skill and perseverance, but they are frequently captured in traps. The flesh of the bandicoot is very white and delicate. Cooked like a rabbit, it furnishes the sportsman's table with a splendid dish.

The WATER MOLE is a most extraordinary little animal. It is usually about a foot and a half long, with the body stout, but somewhat depressed in form and tapering towards the extremities. The head is small, and is provided with a beak somewhat resembling that of a duck. Its feet are webbed, and are each provided with five claws. The male having in addition a large spur similar to that of a game cock upon each of the hinder feet. Its tail is short, broad, and depressed. The fur is of a brown color, very fine, close, and soft to the touch. The water moles burrow in the steep banks of a stream, near their favourite haunts, which are the open and tranquil pools, where there is a good growth of aquatic plants. In some localities of this description they are very numerous, but are so timid and wary that they are only to be shot by the exercise of great caution. The burrow has usually two entrances, one below and one above the surface of the water, both of which communicate with a narrow serpentine passage, generally from twenty to thirty feet in length, terminating in an oval chamber sufficiently capacious for the old and young water moles, and made comfortable by a bedding of dry river weeds. When in the burrow—which an aborigine can usually tell by examining its entrance—these animals can be captured by laying open the passage, but they are more often shot in the water, and brought ashore by a dog. They seldom remain on the surface many minutes, but can easily be seen. Unless the sportsman is concealed, however, and is very noiseless in his movements, they disappear the instant he levels his gun. But if he remains still, they will speedily reappear at a very short distance from where they went down, and if, in the meantime, the sportsman has kept his gun pointed towards the direction in which their rising might be calculated upon, he will get a fair shot. They are often taken in nets, and with the exercise of due skill and caution this would probably be the best mode of capturing them.

The whole of the six families of animals last

mentioned belong to the marsupiata or pouched order.

There are several other small quadrupeds, including a burrowing or prairie rat, which, at certain seasons and in certain localities, constitutes the chief animal food of the natives. None of these, however, are of any value to the sportsman or settler.

BATS.

Of the bat family there is one kind which, although a great pest to the growers of fruit, is frequently of much value to those who traverse the wilderness. This is the FLYING FOX—an animal whose sole resemblance to the quadruped after which he is named is in the color of his skin. This is a very large animal of its class, its body being usually about a foot long, and proportionately stout. It has a great expanse of wing, measuring frequently when spread about three feet from tip to tip. The flying foxes are exceedingly numerous, and sometimes, in the fruit season, make sad havoc. They are, consequently, shot down without mercy. Their flesh is delicate, and they are almost invariably very fat; but owing to the demoniac appearance of their black leathery wings, and to the prejudice which this appearance excites, they are seldom eaten by the settlers. Travellers, however, are frequently indebted for a hearty meal to their success in bringing down these creatures.

They are generally found in flocks and are easily shot. They fly about in search of food after nightfall. During the day they search out a remote place, where they hang in thick clusters from the trees.

BIRDS.

First in size and in rank among the birds of Australia is the EMU. This is one of the family which may be termed winglass, and of which the ostrich ' is generally considered as the head; for the wings of the Australian bird, like those of the ostrich, are mere arms or fins, wholly insufficient to raise it from the ground. They are, however, a considerable aid to the animal when running, which it does with great swiftness. The emu is usually about five or six feet in height, but sometimes much taller. The feathers are of a brown color, fine but wiry and brittle. The plumage near the tail, however, is long and graceful. The flesh of the emu is excellent, resembling good beef, and is dressed in a similar manner. The fat, of which a comparatively large quantity is found adhering to the skin, yields, when melted, a tasteless and almost scentless oil, of a light yellowish color, which is used by bushmen with great advantage as an anti-rheumatic. In the wilds large numbers of the emu are met with, but they retreat before the advance of the white man. In the squatting districts they are still numerous.

The emu is usually hunted with dogs. Those which are accustomed to this work spring at the bird's neck, and despatch it at once, but young and untrained dogs sometimes get near its heels, in which case they are apt to get severely injured, if not killed ; for the emu kicks like a horse. In places where the protection of trees enables the sportsman to approach within convenient range, the emu may be easily brought down by a ball. The natives have a plan of capturing the emu by fencing round the water hole, leaving only a single narrow entrance by which it can approach to drink, so that by watching its motions and by the exercise of due care and caution it may be blocked in and captured or speared before it can effect its escape.

The emu lays about a dozen large eggs, of a dark green color, which, although somewhat strong in flavor are frequently eaten by bushmen with great gusto.

This bird is easily tamed, and its presence is a very suitable and graceful feature in an Australian park. The emu is very hardy, and like his relative the ostrich, has a stomach capable of digesting anything.

The bird next in size to the emu is the CASSOWARY. The first specimen obtained of this bird was procured by Mr. Thomas Wall, naturalist of the late expedition commanded by Mr. Kennedy. This was shot near Cape York, in one of those almost inaccessible gullies which abound in that part of the Australian continent. The Cassowary stands, when erect, between four and five feet high. The head is without feathers, but covered with a blue skin; and, like the emu, it is almost without wings, having mere rudiments. The body is thickly covered with strong dark brown wiry feathers. On the head is a large protuberance of a bright red color, and to the neck are attached, like bells, six or eight round fleshy balls of bright blue and scarlet, which give to the bird a very beautiful appearance. This first, and indeed only specimen of the Australian Cassowary, was unfortunately left at Weymouth Bay, and has not been recovered. Mr. Wall being anxious for its preservation had secured it in a canvas bag, and carried it with him to the spot where, unfortunately for himself and for science, he was lost. In the ravine where this bird was killed, as well as other deep and stony valleys of that neighbourhood, they were seen running in companies of seven or eight. On that part of the north-eastern coast, therefore, they are probably plentiful, and will be met with in all the deep gullies at the base of high hills. The flesh of this bird was eaten, and was found to be delicious; a single leg affording more substantial food than ten or twelve hungry men could dispose of at one meal. The cassowary possesses great strength in its legs, and makes use of this strength in the same manner as the emu. Their whole build, however, is more strong and heavy than that of the latter bird. They are very wary, but their presence may be easily detected by their utterance of a peculiarly loud note, which is taken up and echoed along the gullies; and it would be easy to kill them with a rifle.

The BUSTARD, better known by the erroneous name of the Wild Turkey, ranks next in size and importance to the emu and the cassowary. This bird is an inhabitant of the plains in the interior. It is larger and heavier than the domestic turkey. Its plumage is by no means brilliant, the colors being an olive brown, black, and white. The bustard is provided with a membraneous pouch or bag to hold water, by which means it is enabled to traverse the wide plains and deserts of the interior, far removed from the streams and waterholes. These birds are invariably found in pairs. They are, however, very shy and difficult to approach by a person on foot. A horseman they will allow to come much nearer to them. They may also be approached by following in the wake of cattle, and this latter plan is often resorted to. A pedestrian, however, without any of these precautions, may easily bring them down with a good rifle. The bustard affords to the sportsman a splendid dish.

The BRUSH TURKEY is, as its name imports, an inhabitant of the dense brushes. Its general size is about equal to that of the common and domesticated guinea fowl. Its color is black, its head bare of feathers, and that of the male is provided with orange and red fleshy wattles. Unlike the bustard, this bird is easily shot—it keeps close in the thickets until started by the aid of a dog; when aroused, however, it usually flies to some tree near at hand, and gazes about stupidly until it is knocked over by a shot. The flesh is very delicate, and owing to the ease with which it may be procured, the brush turkey speedily disappears before the advance of population. They are still numerous, however, in many parts of the country There are several different species of this bird, of which one, a very beautiful specimen, has lately been procured by Hugh Gordon, Esq., at the head of the Shoalhaven River, in the county of St. Vincent, and presented by that gentleman to the Australian Museum. One of the most remarkable characteristics of this bird is the process to which it resorts for bringing forth its young. With dry leaves and grasses it first forms a circle, and within this the female lays her eggs, covering and bedding them in with similar materials to those which compose the outer circle. Other birds come and lay their eggs at the same place, covering them up in like manner. Thus a complete mound is often erected, and the eggs within are hatched by the heat generated from the decomposition of the vegetable matter which surrounds them. Whether the parent birds can recognise their separate broods, or take the "callow young" indiscriminately in sets, as they come forth, it it is impossible to say. The eggs are larger than those of the common turkey, and being of excellent flavor, the discovery of one of these mounds is a perfect god-send to the bushman, although a sad detriment to the race of brush-turkeys and to the future success of the sportsman.

Of the QUAIL there are numerous varieties in Australia; more numerous, perhaps, than in any other part of the world. The ordinary quail, which is rather larger than that of England, is plentiful in the vicinity of Sydney, and it is no uncommon thing for a good sportsman to kill from twenty to thirty brace in a single day. The quails are migratory, and vast flocks of them are often found in the sequestered nooks about the coast and its vicinity. They are easily domesticated, and are frequently bred and reared in our aviaries.

The SNIPE is one of the most punctual visitors of the neighbourhood of Sydney, appearing regularly and in vast numbers early in September. There are but two species known here—the common and the painted snipe. The former bird is much like the snipe of England, but larger. The latter closely resembles the painted snipe of India, and is much more scarce than the first-named species.

Of PIGEONS there are a greater variety in Australia than in any other country on earth. From one extremity of New South Wales to the other they are to be met with in vast numbers. The handsomest of the class is the magnificent green or fruit pigeon, of which Wollongong is the most favorite haunt;

occasionally, however, it is met with in gardens near Sydney.* It feeds chiefly on wild figs. Of all the pigeons the wonga wonga is the most admired for the extreme delicacy of its flesh. It is a large bird, but comparatively scarce and difficult to shoot. The most common kind is the bronze wing, so called from the metallic lustre of its plumage. These are numerous even in the brush and scrub lands about Sydney.

All the rivers and lagoons of the interior abound with water fowl. The BITTERN, which in the palmy days of falconry furnished a greatly admired dish, and which even at present is much esteemed in Europe, is commonly met on the Parramatta River, and at other places near Sydney. It is not much eaten here, however, on account of its feeding on small snakes, lizards, and such like animals; although to those who entertain no prejudice against the bittern on this account, its flesh is excellent.

The BLACK SWAN is numerous enough in the more secluded waters, but has disappeared from the vicinity of Sydney. Of GEESE, DUCKS, and TEAL, there are a great variety, and on most of the rivers and lagoons a little removed from the common haunts of men, they may be shot

* It is frequently met with in the grounds of Mr. W. S. M Loay at Elizabeth B y. The beautifully kept and extensive gardens of this gentleman, in fact, are much resorted to by many of the migratory and other birds which elsewhere are comparatively rare.

in considerable numbers. There are varieties of these birds which perch on trees. Ducks are frequently killed by the aborigines with their boomerangs; it is believed, in fact, that the boomerang originated in the necessity of having some implement which would pass before the retreating birds, fly back, and in the event of its not striking any of them on its return flight, would quietly deposit itself near the feet of its owner.*

PELICANS of large size are numerous not only in the vicinity of the coast, but on the rivers of the interior; they are very fat, and yield a comparatively large quantity of good animal oil, as much as a quart being sometimes procured from a single bird; the neck, breast, wings, and legs, are good eating, but the body of the bird has a strong and fishy flavor.

CRANES are also very numerous. The native companion, a tall, handsome, and majestic bird, is of this species, and is most easily domesticated. It is a matter of surprise indeed that they are not more frequently met with in the farm yards and grounds of the colonists. Of the SPOONBILL and IBIS there are many species, the

---

* It is generally known, we believe, that the boomerang is a flattened piece of wood, curved in the form of an obtuse angle, and partially sharpened at the edge; which, when cast by the aborigine, first proceeds with a whirling motion to a considerable distance, and then turning back upon its course, falls near the spot from which it was thrown. There are some boomerangs, however, which are used in war, that are somewhat different in model, and do not return to the thrower.

sacred ibis of the Egyptians, or a bird very nearly allied to it, being included among the latter family. Some of the birds belonging to these three families are very beautiful.

The RED BILL, found principally near the sea coast, is a bird much resembling the English Coot, but is larger. It is plump and fine flavored. RAILS, WATER HENS, PLOVERS, and CURLEWS, are also numerous. The bird which is usually called the curlew by the colonists, is in reality a plover, remaining close all day, and at night seeking its food with a loud mewing cry, forming a very disagreeable serenade to young colonists.

Of sea GULLS there are but two varieties — the large grey or black-backed gull, and the common red legged species found in nearly all parts of the world. They may be easily shot in the waters of Port Jackson. The ALBATROSS and PETREL are common in the adjacent seas, and the SOLAN GOOSE is, in bad weather, a frequent visitor, even within the harbour. This bird is excellent food when salted. The small gulls are also good food, but the larger are somewhat strong.

COCKATOOS are of many kinds. For the most part, however, they are so well known as to need no description. These are all excellent eating. The common white cockatoos, although met with in large flocks, are very wary, and are consequently difficult to shoot. They generally perch, if practicable, upon a dead and bare tree, the upper bird keeping a sharp look out around, and giving the alarm the moment he sees the sportsman approaching. By advancing cautiously, however, under cover of the bushes when any are at hand, much havoc may frequently be made among one of these flocks ; for if a bird is wounded so that he will cry out lustily, without being able to get away, the others will hover about the spot and stand a good deal of "peppering." The black cockatoo is a splendid bird, and is more easily shot than the white variety ; but it has never, we believe, been found possible to domesticate one of them.

PARROTS are of all Australian birds the most numerous, and as a class the best known. The number of varieties in this family, however, is astonishingly great, and the catalogue is still increasing, for the discovery of a new species of parrot is a circumstance of frequent occurrence. All the Australian parrots have handsome plumage ; some of them indeed are extremely magnificent in the variety, the brilliancy, and the disposition of their colors. That kind which is generally known in the colony as the "blue mountaineer" or the "blue mountains' parrot," is distinguished by plumage so beautiful and brilliant that if it was a scarce bird there can be no doubt it would be greatly sought after and as greatly prized when taken. It is however, an exceedingly common bird, and, as a natural consequence, it is, comparatively speaking, but little cared for. Great numbers of these birds, as well as of smaller parrots, are shot near Sydney. But the dwellers in the suburbs have discovered a much more easy way of supplying themselves with blue mountaineers than by searching for them with a gun. A young sapling or a limb from a tree of larger growth is fixed in the ground, and near its summit is suspended a cage containing one or two parrots. Upon the branches above and around this cage are affixed small running nooses of fine wire or hair. The noise of the captive birds attracts their wild companions, who alight near the cage to see what is the matter, and one if not more of each party, almost invariably manages to put either its head or one of its feet into one of the nooses. From this position it is speedily released by the bird catcher, and removed to the cage to increase the noise of its occupants and decoy some more of their companions. The number of birds taken in this way is truly astonishing. Some of our juveniles will by this simple contrivance get a tolerably large cage full in the course of a few hours. It is this kind and a smaller green parrot, commonly known as the green paroquet, which are usually captured for the purpose of domestication and training; the latter kind being the most docile and teachable of the two. Few of the parrot kind are particularly shy or wary, and in the forests where they abound they afford excellent sport. In fact the mode in which parrots are occasionally brought down and the number of them that are secured is scarcely credible to those who have never indulged in this kind of shooting. In traversing a piece of rich open forest land the sportsman will frequently arrive at a good spreading and thickly branched tree on which a number of parrots, usually of the smaller green kind, are feeding, and if he has shot of a convenient size in his belt (No. 6 is about the best for this kind of service) he may usually bring them down as long as he chooses to load and fire. His own patience is more likely to be exhausted than that of the parrots. They will start from the tree, indeed, at every shot, but they will generally return to it at once, and other birds, attracted probably by the squalling of their wounded brethern, will arrive at the scene of slaughter; and this kind of game is by no means despicable, for parrots large and small are capital eating, either curried, stewed, or in a pie.

The GILL BIRD, wattle bird, or honey sucker, also makes its appearance in large flocks near Sydney, about the month of May, and affords a good deal of sport to the youthful gunners of the metropolis; it is a sober looking bird, rather larger than an English thrush, and has derived two of its names from certain " gills " or "wattles" with which it is provided. The flesh is very delicate and well flavoured. The FRIAR BIRD, so called from its bald head, is about the size of the gill bird, and although not met with in such large numbers as the latter, is a frequent and acceptable aid in filling up the game bag or the pockets of the Sydney sportsman.

We have now, we believe, enumerated all the birds which are ordinarily shot or otherwise captured for food; but others are occasionally used by bushmen, and to the aborigines nothing comes amiss. The MAGPIE, which is a large and handsome bird, everywhere abundant, is sometimes sought for the table; but is more generally captured alive in order that it may be trained as a "family musician," an office for which its melodious whistling note and the facility with which it can acquire an air, especially qualify it. The common CROW is very grateful food to an aboriginal palate, but owing the partiality of this bird to carrion, few white men ever taste it. Such of them as have done so, declare that a pie made of young crows is fully equal to one composed of young rooks; and the latter is a well-known and favorite dish in England.

Birds of prey are, also, as numerous and varied in kind as the smaller and weaker species of the feathered races. The WEDGE-TAILED EAGLE is the largest of this class; but the most common of the eagle family is the bird called by the colonists the EAGLE HAWK, some of which are sufficiently large and powerful to carry off young lambs. Of FALCONS there are many varieties, some of them very beautiful. Among these is one very closely allied to the PEREGRINE FALCON, so much esteemed by the lovers of

G

falcony in Europe. Birds of the rapacious order, which seek their prey in he waters, are also common. The WHITE BELLIED SEA EAGLE, which is the largest of this class, may be frequently seen dashing into the waters of the har. our and carrying off a large mullet, bream, or other fish to its eyrie. Sometimes it will strike its claws into a fish so large that the struggles of the captive will bring it frequently to the water, nay, sometimes will plunge it fairly in before it can obtain a complete victory. It is but seldom however that the fish escapes. The smaller birds of prey—the hawks and the buzzards, are very numerous, and the owls are as fully and fairly represented as the rest.

We have heard it said, nay we have seen the assertion in print, that the woods and meadows of Australia are destitute of singing birds. No assertion can be more erroneous. All who have lived in " the bush" and have been accustomed to rise with the sun can bear testimony to the fact that we have a full and fair supply of those feathered choristers whose presence gives life and cheerfulness to the wilderness. There is a small brown bird, one of the class termed warblers, which has a note equal, if not superior, to that of the English nightingale. Unhappily it is scarce. But there are many kinds of songsters which may be more frequently met with. Of these, the LYRE BIRD has the first rank. Its own note is good, but its chief excellence is in its extraordinary powers of imitation. There is scarcely a sound which this bird will not imitate to perfection, and some imagine that the little mimic takes a pride in the exercise of its deceptive powers. The lyre-bird is small, and there is nothing remarkable in its plumage with the exception of the tail, from the form of which it derives its name. This is unusually long, with two large and finely marked feathers curling outwards at their extremities in the form of a lyre. These birds are most commonly found in deep gullies and heavy brush lands, and are very numerous in the district of Illawarra. A second species has been observed by Dr. Bennett,* whose reputation as a naturalist stands deservedly high ; the chief variation being that the large tail feathers of this latter kind have an inward instead of an outward curve at their extremities. It was discovered at the Richmond River. Besides the songster first mentioned, there are many of the warblers which sing very melodiously. A small blue wren, also, which is common enough in the gardens around Sydney, has a sweet although short note. No attempt, that we are aware of, has ever been made to domesticate any of these Australian songsters.

* This was discovered by a Mr. Stephenson ; and a Mr. Leycester being the first who suggested the probability of its being a new species, it was proposed to name it after that gentleman. Mr. Goold, however, to whom a specimen was sent, has named it after H. R. H. Prince Albert.

There are many Australian birds which, although not properly describable as songsters, are distinguished by a singularity of note. The most remarkable of these is the ORGAN BIRD or ventriloquist ; it gives utterance to three distinct and bell-like notes, following each other in quick succession, but possess the singular power of making these sounds appear to proceed from various points considerably removed from the place where it is actually perched. We have heard of a naturalist being led a terrible dance in search of one of these little deceivers, when in reality it was pouring forth its notes but a short distance from the spot from which he started ; the only certain way of getting hold of it is by imitating its cry, when it comes to the spot to have a look at its supposed neighbour. The COACH WHIP BIRD, frequently heard but seldom seen in the neighbourhood of Sydney, derives its name from its utterance of a sound very similar to the cracking of a small whip. The DISH WASHER or wagtail, also common in the vicinity of Sydney, is remarkable for its indulgence in a peculiar cry of gratification, half humming, half grunting, whenever it has captured a fly or any other of the small insects upon which it feeds. The LAUGHING JACKASS, a large and coarse looking bird, with dark plumage, which is pretty common every where, gives utterance to most extraordinary sounds. Generally they are of a kind perfectly indescribable, but sometimes they resemble so much a loud derisive laugh as to grate with peculiar harshness upon the ear of the juvenile sportsman when roaming unsuccessfully in search of game. The unlucky bird sometimes pays with its life for the infliction of this annoyance, but as it generally selects a high perch, it more frequently escapes scathless from the shot of the irate juvenile, in which case, whilst removing to a safer distance, it usually expresses its alarm by giving utterance to a laugh of more than usual power, which in no way consoles the unsuccessful shooter. Old colonists never kill these birds, for they are totally unfit for the table, and they are really of great service, inasmuch as they pursue and destroy the venomous snakes, which, in all parts of the bush are but too numerous. The laughing jackass has also earned for itself the title of the bushman's clock, from its usefulness, like chanticleer, in arousing him to his labour at early dawn.

There are a large number of birds, besides those already mentioned, which are valuable on account of the extreme beauty of their plumage, such as the rifle bird, the regent bird, the dragoon bird, the diamond bird, &c. Of the robin, finch, wren, and other families, there are also many and very splendidly colored varieties, some of which may occasion- be seen in our aviaries, although they are far less sought for and prized than they deserve to be.

THE CROCODILE.

The crocodile or alligator is an inhabitant of all the northern rivers; at Port Essington and in the waters around it, these creatures are exceedingly numerous, and Mr. Kennedy's party saw a very large one on the beach at Rockingham Bay; they may yet perhaps be found still further south. The Australian animal is closely allied to the gavial or crocodile of India, but is more often termed, like the American species, an alligator. It is large and formidable, one captured by Captain Stokes, in the Victoria River, and described in his published journal, was fifteen feet long; and some have been taken still larger than this. Like all animals of its class, the Australian crocodile is a much more formidable enemy in the water than on shore, but even in the latter position, it is by no means to be despised, for it progresses with tolerable speed, and although it seldom or never attacks a man openly when out of its own proper element, still it is believed to have a strong liking for human flesh, when that delicacy can safely be obtained. One of these creatures paid a visit to a seaman, who was asleep in his hammock on shore after a hard day's labor, and being unable to get conveniently at the man, it managed to drag off and carry away the blanket which covered him; the sailor at first charged his comrades with having made him the subject of a practical joke, but the foot prints of the huge reptile, and the discovery of the abstracted blanket in the water, soon shewed him the real character of his nocturnal visitant.

The flesh of the crocodile is white and delicate, resembling veal. It was a favorite dish among the Port Essington settlers, and among the seamen employed in the surveys of the northern coast and rivers ; and is frequently pursued and killed for food by the aborigines of that part of the country. The plan which they adopt is to hunt it into some blind creek, when the reptile finding itself closely pressed and no water near, usually forces its head and perhaps the upper part of its body into some sandhole, fancying that it has by so doing concealed itself from its pursuers. In this position it is despatched with comparative ease. The crocodile makes a terrible noise by snapping its jaws, particularly when in pain or when it is annoyed by the buzzing about its mouth and eyes of the mosquitoes and other insects, which are found in myriads among the swamps, creeks, and shallow waters, where it abides ; this snapping noise is often a startling sound to explorers encamping near waters frequented by the monster.

The aboriginal tribes far to the southward of the localities in which the crocodile has its habitation, have an imperfect knowledge of the animal. Stories of its voracity and fierceness have probably been recounted at the friendly meetings of the tribes, and these

H

stories have in the same manner passed across the continent, changed and magnified with each new-relation, until on reaching the coast tribes of the south, the crocodile became a nondescript animal of most terrible form, frightening the blacks and puzzling the whites under the name of the Bunyip.

IGUANAS AND LIZARDS.

The IGUANA, or, as it is more commonly termed in New South Wales, the GOUANA, is very frequently met with. There are several varieties of this reptile, but that which is most common is from four to six feet in length, and from about a foot and a half to two feet across the broadest part of the back, with a rough dark skin, enlivened by yellow spots. This huge lizard is a very formidable looking animal, but it is perfectly harmless as far as the human race are concerned, although a terrible foe to the smaller quadrupeds—opossums, bandicoots, kangaroo-rats, &c.,—on which it preys. It is very destructive, also, among hen roosts, and often takes up its quarters in the vicinity of a farm house for the convenience of supping on the hens and their eggs.

The gouana is much sought for and esteemed by the blacks as an article of food, and is frequently presented as a great delicacy to the young gins. By the settlers it is not often eaten, owing to the natural feeling of dislike which is created by its form and habits. Those, however, who do not entertain these feelings, or are able to overcome them, find the flesh of the creature really excellent. It is not unlike that of a rabbit, to which, in flavor, it is fully equal, and eats best when stewed or curried.

The gouana usually lives in trees, and on the approach of man it invariably makes off with great alacrity, scrambling rapidly up the nearest trunk, but it is easily brought down by a shot.

There are an almost innumerable variety of lizards, properly so called, in all parts of the colony, and the whole of the larger kinds are used for food by the blacks, although but very rarely eaten by the settlers. Those who have eaten them, state that their flesh resembles that of a fowl. The DRAGON LIZARD, or as it is sometimes called the FRILLED LIZARD, is the most remarkable, being provided with a large frill, which it has the power of extending suddenly, and in a rather startling manner, when attacked or alarmed ; it is usually about a foot and a half or two feet long. The JEW LIZARDS are dark coloured with a dewlapped and puffy appearance about the throat and neck, varying in size, but seldom exceeding two feet in length. The SCALY LIZARDS are fierce looking, although harmless reptiles, with a spotted scaly hide, generally about a foot long, and remarkable for having small round club-shaped tails. They are easily domesticated, but as their appearance is far from attractive, they are seldom made pets of. The large

SPINY-BACKED ROCK LIZARD resembles a gouana, the only material points of difference being that it has a heavy dewlap beneath its chin, and a row of spines along the back from the head to the tail. The FLAT-TAILED LIZARD, called by the natives the rock scorpion, is imagined by them to be venomous, although in reality it is perfectly harmless ; it is nocturnal in its habits, and possesses to a peculiar extent the singular power, which is more or less vested in all the lizard family, of leaving its tail in the hands of any one who attempts to capture it by laying hold of that appendage, and of making off apparently scatheless. The SLEEPING LIZARD is in body, as well as in its sluggish habits, exactly like the terrible death adder, from which it is only to be distinguished by its short feet.

Many of the lizard family are believed by the settlers to be venomous, but such is not the case ; we believe, in fact, that no four footed reptile has yet been discovered which is possessed of venom.

A remarkable power possessed by the gouana, and perhaps by others of the lizard family, is its power of resisting the poison, ordinarily most destructive to animal life— prussic acid. A middling sized gouana took a small bottle of prussic acid, and seemed rather to have been exhilirated by it than otherwise ; it was killed however by a dose of arsenic and spirits of wine.

The skins of the gouana and of most of the

larger lizards, are very tough and may be usefully applied to all the purposes for which shagreen is used ; belts and pouches are, however, we believe, the only articles which have yet been made of them, and these have usually been manufactured in a very primitive manner, by the bushmen who have killed the reptiles.

The small nimble-footed lizards which swarm in all parts of the bush, although occasionally hunted up and captured by the natives when hard pressed for food, cannot be said to be of any practical use to the settler, except in the continuous and destructive war which they wage against insects.

TURTLES AND TORTOISES.

This class of amphibious animals are largely represented both upon the coasts and in the rivers and swamps of the interior. The large GREEN TURTLE—the honored food of civic dignitaries in the mother country—abounds on the northern and north-eastern coasts. It is seldom found near Sydney, but the dwellers in the metropolis are supplied by the steamer and trading vessels which run to Moreton Bay. Gigantic specimens of this animal, at which a London alderman would gaze with mixed feelings of astonishment and delight, are so frequently seen lying upon the pavement outside some of our hotels that few passengers bestow upon them more than a passing and careless glance. The prices of turtle in the Sydney market vary, of course, with the supply and demand, but in spite of the inconvenience and increased expense of bringing them from a place distant several days' voyage, and notwithstanding the additional charges for cookery and hotel-keepers' profit, a citizen of Sydney may, for a single shilling, lunch off green turtle, and enjoy "calipash and calipee" superior in flavor and freshness to any which makes its appearance upon a London board. The HAWK's-BILLED TURTLE, which produces the well-known tortoise-shell of commerce, is also caught upon the northern and north-eastern coasts, but, as yet, it has not been much sought for.

Of fresh-water turtles, or TORTOISES, there are several varieties. About the Murrumbidgee and other rivers of the interior they are found of considerable size—some from a foot and a half to two feet in length—but they are usually less than half that size. The smaller kinds are frequently taken in the Botany swamps, within a mile or two of the city, especially after heavy rains.

The whole of these species are esteemed good food by the blacks, but are seldom, if ever, eaten by the settlers. In Russia, however, and in some parts of Germany, the fresh water turtles are fattened for the table, and are esteemed a very great delicacy. Some of these animals, and in particular the larger kinds, have the power of putting forth a very disagreeable exhalation when first captured, so as to make the carrying of them an unpleasant task. The shells of all these small tortoises are, we believe, useless.

SNAKES.

Of these reptiles many species are to be met with in all parts of the colony and some of them are but too numerous. The majority of the Australian snakes are more or less venomous, but they are, as a family, by no means so dangerous as they are reputed to be. With the exception of the dreaded death adder, the water snakes, which are occasionally met with on the coast and in the rivers of the interior, and a small brown species, there is none of them possessed of venom sufficiently virulent to occasion death if the most ordinary care and promptitude be exercised in the application of remedies, and the bite of even the most deadly may be readily cured if proper measures are taken on the instant.

The largest individual of this great family of reptiles which is found in New South Wales is the DIAMOND SNAKE. Although formerly reputed to be a venomous serpent, and still bearing that character among some of the settlers, the diamond snake is perfectly harmless, destroying its prey by strangulation like the boa-constrictor. It is marked with black and yellow spots in a diamond or lozenge shape, and hence its name. Its ordinary length is from eight to ten feet, but, occasionally, it is found much larger. There is a very fine specimen in the Sydney Museum, twelve feet in length, which was presented by the late Sir George Gipps; it was killed in the neighbourhood of Cook's River, while in the act of swallowing a full grown opossum, which was subsequently taken from its stomach and is now set up along with the snake in the Museum.

The CARPET SNAKE greatly resembles the foregoing in size, habits, and general aspect, but its skin is marked with irregular brown and yellow stripes or patches. It has no venom.

The BLACK SNAKE, which is frequently met with near Sydney, and is common, indeed, throughout the entire country, is the largest of the poisonous snakes. Its bite has sometimes occasioned loss of life, but is not necessarily mortal, and could only have proved so in consequence of proper remedies not having been applied, or of the extreme terror and nervousness which the conviction of having received a mortal wound has naturally bred in the mind of the person bitten. This snake is of a dull black colour on the back, with a reddish belly, generally about four or five feet long, but occasionally much larger. It is very active in its habits, and although it will always fly from man, it is very bold and vindictive when assailed. To the smaller animals upon which this reptile preys its bite is certain death.

Of the BROWN SNAKE there are four

varieties, two of which are venomous, and two harmless. The largest of these seldom exceeds four or five feet in length. A brown snake four feet five inches long was brought some time back to the Curator of the Sydney Museum, and on dissecting it a second brown snake of another species, four feet six inches long, was found in its stomach. It is clear, therefore, that these venomous reptiles prey upon each other, and but for this circumstance they would probably be still more numerous than they are.

The WHIP SNAKE is long and slender, deriving its name from its supposed resemblance to the lash of a whip. It is of a greenish tint. Its habits are active, and, as it flies from man, it seldom does much injury, although its bite is poisonous.

Of WATER SNAKES there are several varieties, and they are all exceedingly venomous, but they are happily not very numerous, and we have never heard any well authenticated instance of a person being bitten by an Australian water snake. Ordinarily they are small, but some of them, especially those which inhabit the ocean, are of a large size. One of them, which was discovered by Captain Stokes, and which has been well and truly described as the giant of this class, had a body as thick as a man's thigh. Most of the ordinary snakes, and particularly the black kind, are occasionally seen in the water, where they swim with great ease and speed, and are frequently taken for water snakes. The true water snakes, however, may be easily distinguished from all others by their possessing a flattened tail, similar to that of an eel.

The RING SNAKE is small, marked by alternate circles of black and white, and is nocturnal in its habits. The GREEN SNAKE and the BLUISH-GREY SNAKE are also of small size. There are other small varieties of the snake family which it is unnecessary to describe in detail, some venomous and some harmless, but none deadly. The SAND SNAKE, which is more commonly known as the slow worm, is frequently met with near Sydney, and, although perfectly harmless, has acquired the reputation of being peculiarly venomous. When alarmed this snake has the power of contracting and stiffening itself in an extraordinary manner. When in this state it is singularly brittle, and by a very slight blow may be broken up like a piece of glass or china ; it often loses its tail by accidents which occur to it while in its contracted state, but it is speedily furnished with a new one. There is one of this species, with two tails, in the Sydney Museum.

We now come to the DEATH ADDER. This is a truly venomous reptile, well worthy of the terrible and expressive name by which it is now known, although originally and properly called the Deaf Adder from the sluggishness of its habits, occasioned, as is popularly believed, by its inability to hear the sound of

approaching footsteps. It is most disgusting
and repulsive in its aspect, and is at once recognised most easily even by those who have
never before seen it. It is seldom more than
two feet and a half in length, but is of more
than ordinary thickness, and does not taper
gradually towards the extremities like other
snakes. It has, however, a little hardened
and sting-like tail, with which it is generally
supposed to have the power of inflicting a
wound as deadly as its bite. This, however,
is a mere error. The tail, at least, is harmless;
although it assists the snake in springing at an
assailant. This reptile is of a dusky brown
colour, with numerous grey spots, and its
general appearance is not much unlike
that of a dried branch, for which it may
at a casual glance be easily mistaken as
it lies stretched motionless on the
earth. The death adder never moves aside to
avoid the approaching pedestrian, but, on the
other hand, it is never the assailant. Unless
it is fairly trod upon or struck at, it sdeadly
fangs are never called into requisition. It is
consequently easily avoided, and as easily
destroyed. The only risk is that of treading
upon it accidentally, or of striking at and
missing it. Its poison is very deadly in its
operation, and diffuses itself so rapidly
throughout the system, that the life of any
person who has been bitten by it can only be
preserved by immediate and decisive applications of a remedial nature.

One species of brown snake is believed to be almost as destructive as the death adder, but it is from the bite of the latter reptile that most casualties of this nature have taken place. Death, however, has ensued not only from the bite of snakes whose venom is not so virulent as necessarily to prove fatal when infused into the system, but even from the bite of snakes which are now known to have no venom whatever. This result can only be accounted for by ascribing it to the powerful operation of the mind upon the body. The bite of a snake, particularly if it be a large one, will, like that of most other animals, cause some inflammation and pain. This of itself alarms the person who has been bitten, but when the terrors of approaching death are added, the mind and nerves become so fearfully excited that these fears bring about their own fulfilment. We have heard of persons suffering an agony of terror, and exhibiting many of the symptoms of a snake bite, when in reality they have only been stung by some of the small prickly plants which are found in the bush, or nipped by a large ant; the true and only cause of their pain and annoyance being their belief that it was in reality the teeth of a venomous snake which they had felt.

Any snake by which a person has been bitten is usually killed. In this case, it is very easy to discover whether it is venomous or harmless by examining its mouth. The venomous kinds are invariably furnished with additional teeth, sharp, long, and tubular, which are termed the poison fangs. These teeth are connected at their roots with a gland by which the poison is secreted, and from whence it is instilled into the wound through the hollow of the fang. As a general rule, the virulence of a snake's poison is diminished, in proportion to the activity of the reptile's habits The snakes which have no venom are stronger in the jaws, and better furnished with teeth than those which are provided with this means of offence. Hence the bite of a harmless snake is to a person unacquainted with its nature, far more startling than the scarcely perceptible wound which has infused into the system a deadly animal poison; any one who has been bitten, should therefore satisfy himself that there is real danger before he allows his fears to get the better of his reason and confidence. Where there is any doubt, however, it is always safest and best to adopt precautionary measures.

The bite from a venomous Australian serpent does not ordinarily, like that of the rattlesnake and some other poisonous serpents, cause any immediate change in the appearance of the skin around the wound, nor does it produce much bodily pain. The poison operates by dispersing itself rapidly through the nervous system, and causes the person bitten to fall into a state of stupor, impairing greatly his powers of vision, of smell, and of taste, although usually without affecting his consciousness.

When a person has been bitten by a poisonous snake, a handkerchief or some other ligature should be tied round the limb immediately above the wound, so tightly as to stop, as far as possible, the circulation of the blood. An incision should then be made on either side of the punctures from the fangs of the snake to a depth a little below that to which these fangs have penetrated, and the intervening flesh cut fairly out. To do this requires some nerve, but a man has only to bear in mind that this course is absolutely necessary for the preservation of his life, and he will cut boldly enough. The blood should be allowed to flow freely from the gash thus made, and if there is any one at hand to suck the wound, this precaution should be taken. This may be done without the slightest fear, for the poison of a snake is only dangerous when infused into the veins through a wound. It is better, indeed, that any person who thus extracts the venom from a snake bite should wash his mouth out occasionally with salad oil if at hand, but this is by no means absolutely necessary. The aborigines readily suck out the poison infused by a snake bite without any such precaution as this, and without sustaining any inconvenience. If any nitric acid can be procured, and about half a dozen drops of it applied to the wound it will materially aid the cure. The wound, having been thus enlarged and purged, a poultice of ipecacuanha, if procurable, should be applied without loss of time, but if this is not at hand a poultice of linseed meal or bread and milk may be substituted. In either case it will be well to accompany the external applications with strong internal medicines of a purgative and cleansing nature.

The plan which has been successfully adopted in India for curing the bite of the water snakes, has been to enlarge the wound with a lancet, and to bind in it, with a ligature, a small piece of carbonate of ammonia, well moistened with pure nitric acid, administering internally, at the same instant, thirty drops of eau-de-luce in a glass of water, and repeating the latter dose at intervals of a few minutes, until it produces a violent nausea and profuse perspiration. The following is said to have been found an effectual remedy for the bite of the American rattlesnake, and and might perhaps be used with advantage in Australia. Take equal quantities of the herbs plantain and horehound, gathered when fresh and verdant, and pound them, roots and all, in a mortar, so as to extract their juices. Of the liquor thus obtained, give to the patient a table-spoonfull, applying at the same time some tobacco, moistened with strong spirits, to the wound. If relief is not obtained in the course of an hour, a second dose of the vegetable juices is given. Both the plants alluded to are plentiful enough here.

In all cases of this nature, however, the

wisest and safest course is to call in with all possible speed the aid of a competent medical practitioner, but the operation of the poison infused from the fangs of the venomous snakes is so rapid, that it is absolutely necessary to apply in the mean time the best remedies at hand.

Snakes are eaten by the aborigines, and white men who when very hard pressed have partaken of them, describe the flesh as being very delicate, like that of fowl. Belts are sometimes made from the skins of these reptiles, as a trophy, by those who have destroyed them.

VENOMOUS INSECTS.

The powers and malignity of the venomous insects have been still more greatly magnified than those of the snakes. The centipede, the scorpion, and the tarantula, are too well known to need description ; but although all of them are frequently met with people are but rarely injured by them. The centipede is decidedly the worst of the three, and although its bite is seldom or never fatal, still, if neglected, it will usually produce violent inflammation, if not worse results. Fingers and toes have frequently been lost by neglecting wounds of this nature. The application of ammonia to the wounded part, with purgative medicines taken internally, will usually allay the pain and prevent all permanent injury. If no ammonia is at hand, any strong drawing poultice may be applied.

The large ants bite very severely, but beyond the sharp pang of the instant they inflict no injury.

INSECTS GENERALLY.

For the researches of the entymologist, New South Wales affords an almost boundless field. But beautifully and singularly formed as are many of these little creatures, they do not as a class come properly within the scope of our work ; for we do not profess to give, even in outline, a natural history of the colony. Our object, as was stated at the outset, is simply to impart such information as will prove practically useful to the ordinary settler.

Two insects—a kind of butterfly and a thick white grub, found chiefly in dead timber, are much esteemed by the aborigines as articles of food. The former is eaten at certain seasons by whole tribes of natives in the northern districts. Their practice is to follow up the flight of the insects and to light fires at nightfall beneath the trees in which they have roosted. The smoke brings the butterflies down, and their bodies are pounded together into a sort of fleshy loaf. Upon this delicacy the natives not only feed but fatten. The white grub is swallowed whole in his living state, and is much sought for by sable epicures. It is scarcely necessary to say that neither of these dainties have found favour with the white settlers.

There is a wild bee in all parts of the continent, but these insects are met only in small communities, and their honey, when found, seldom repays the seeker for the trouble and labour of his search, owing to the smallness of the quantity in each nest. Although this honey is sought for by the blacks, the settlers do not indulge in bee hunting. The honey of the Australian wild bee bears a peculiar flavor, imparted chiefly by the flowers of the eucalypti. The European bee, however, is now very common in a wild state, and the honey is of a superior kind.

Among the Australian beetles there are some whose wings, shining with the richest metallic lustre, would be of considerable value in Europe for dress ornaments; but they have not hitherto been sought or used for any such purpose.

FISH.

Of river fish there are but few varieties, but this deficiency is amply compensated for by the numbers and varieties of the finny tribes in the salt water streams in the harbours and in the neighbouring ocean.

A large fish, termed a COD, and resembling the " genuine American," although of a different species, is found in the western waters—the Murray, the Murrumbidgee, &c. PERCHES, similar to those of the European rivers, are also common to those of Australia. There are several other kinds, chiefly small. EELS, however, grow to a considerable size, and are of a peculiarly fine flavor, the very heaviest of them being as delicate as the smallest.

The rapid fall of the waters in the Australian rivers during the summer season, and the frequent drying up of their beds, are natural and obvious impediments to the breeding of fish in these waters. But even for this difficulty nature has, to a certain extent, provided. Fish a few inches long, similar in fact to the well-known "gudgeon" of the English streams, have been found in a torpid state embedded in the soil of the dried creeks two or three feet below the surface, and these, when placed in their native element, have at once started into life and activity in the same manner as if they had been taken from a full and flowing stream.

In the harbours, in the mouths of the larger streams, and in the adjacent ocean, SHARKS of various kinds are very numerous. Several frightful accidents have occurred in consequence of the recklessness with which bathers resort to the waters where these monsters are known to prowl, and considering the extent of this practice it is surprising that many more of these accidents have not occurred. This is chiefly owing to the fact that the large and more dangerous kinds of shark are found almost exclusively in the deeper waters, while the bathers resort to the small and comparatively shallow bays. Sharks are frequently caught when trying, with a large hook, for other fish ; and as two of a trade can never agree, so there is a natural antipathy between the shark and the fisherman, which causes the latter to seek eagerly the destruction of the former. Sharks are even, at times, fished for with strong tackle, in order that they may be destroyed. This, however, is a somewhat difficult matter when a large shark is hooked, but practised fishermen usually carry an axe or tomahawk for contingencies such as these. In the absence of any such weapon the shark is beaten with the oars and stretchers, or pierced with the boat-hook. He frequently manages however, to break through everything and escape. Residents on or near the coast procure a good serviceable oil for their lamps from the fat and liver of the shark, but this oil has a most abominable smell. The shark is never eaten. Fish of the finest flavor are so abundant that all Australians are complete epicures with regard to this species of diet, and besides the shark, which although eaten readily at sea, is coarse and strong in flavor, many kinds really well fitted for the table are rejected.

The SCHNAPPER, a thick hunch-backed fish, usually about a foot and a-half or two feet long, is the one most commonly sought for, and this for two reasons, first, because its flesh is white, firm, and of superior flavor ; and secondly, because being a bold and ready feeder, and plentifully met with on the coast near Sydney, its capture is found more profitable to the fishermen than the capture of smaller prey. Schnappers are seldom taken far up the harbour, but may be procured in large numbers near the Sydney heads and at the reefs outside the entrance. Professional fishermen, and those with whom fishing has been so much practised in the shape of an amusement as to become almost a profession, are acquainted with particular spots where these fish congregate in larger numbers than usual.

The KING FISH and the JEW FISH are also large, resembling the European salmon in size and outward appearance, although not in the color or flavor of their flesh, which is not generally esteemed so much as that of the schnapper. A true COD FISH, closely allied to that caught on the banks of Newfoundland, has recently been discovered, but has not yet found its way into the colonial markets.

There are an innumerable variety of smaller fish in the harbour of Port Jackson, and, consequently, in the bays and estuaries along the coast, to say nothing of those which people the ocean. MULLET, WHITING, MACKAREL, BREAM, SOLES, and GUARD FISH, similar to those known by the same names in Europe, may be especially mentioned, but there are very many others peculiar for the most part to our own waters, and all, or nearly all of them well flavored. Of ROCK FISH also, there are many varieties, those of the ROCK COD—

black and red—being the principal. These are singularly ominous looking fish, having huge heads covered over with spines. They take a bait readily, and are well worth the trouble of their capture, for their flesh is firm, white, and of a peculiarly fine flavour. Large brown snake-like EELS are also caught among the rocks, which, although somewhat startling in their aspect to those who capture them for the first time, are of excellent flavour, and are highly esteemed by the Australian epicures.

The sea CRAY FISH, usually called the lobster by the colonists, are occasionally found of an enormous size and weight on various parts of the coast, and more particularly at Broken Bay (the mouth of the Hawkesbury), from whence the Sydney market is supplied. From four to six pounds, however, is the most common size, and when the weight exceeds this the flesh is inferior. A small variety, found in the fresh water rivers, and really known, by a singular contradiction, as the cray-fish, is in reality more of a lobster, having the large claws which in the sea cray is wanting. CRABS of large size and fine flavor are plentiful on the north-eastern coast, and are occasionally brought to the capital by the Moreton Bay packets. Smaller kinds are very plentiful on the shores of Port Jackson. PRAWNS, some of large size, and all of superior flavor, are plentiful in various localities, and particularly in the River Hunter, from whence they are sent to Sydney.

Of OYSTERS there are three kinds—the rock oyster, the mud oyster, and the pearl oyster. The latter are found to the northward, although as yet but little sought after or cared for. The two former kinds are plentiful everywhere. The mud oysters are of large size, but it is the rock oyster which is most esteemed by the colonists. There is scarcely a stone which is washed by the salt water that is not covered with them, and the supply may be said to be inexhaustible. COCKLES, similar in appearance and equal in flavor to those of England, although of a different species, are to be found in abundance on every earthen flat over which the salt water rises. PERRI-WINKLES, large and small, and other spiral shelled varieties, fully as delicate and as useful for the table as the English "welk," are equally plentiful, although compara-tively but little sought for. MUSCLES are but seldom used for food, except by the natives, although they are of good flavor when partially boiled, after the English fashion. There is a muscle common to the fresh water rivers, which is much sought after and esteemed as food by the aborigines.

The fisherman's craft, as practised in the Australian waters, is simple enough, but an European professor of the "gentle art" has something to learn, or rather, perhaps, to unlearn, before he can be considered proficient.

Angling, as practised in England, is almost unknown here. The number and variety of large fish which may with ease be captured from a boat, causes the Sydney fishermen to look with contempt upon the smaller kinds which may be taken near the shore with a rod and line.

In the rivers, however, this sort of fishing may be resorted to with far greater advantage than the clumsy hand line system which is usually practised; and even upon the coast the angler may, with proper tackle, be certain of very excellent sport. Rod fishing, nevertheless, is practised almost exclusively by boys, and that with the most rude description of tackle. A short and half-crooked branch, torn from the nearest gum-tree, a coarse cotton twist line, with a thick wine cork for a float, and a clumsy hook, still more clumsily fastened, is the general equipment of a juvenile angler; but even with such implements as these, such a number and variety of fish will often in an hour or two be captured, as an English sportsman would gaze at with great satisfaction, even as the result of a day's fishing with the superior skill and the costly apparatus which he has at his command. We have seen a boy, thus equipped, capture " yellow-tail" as fast as he could throw his line. This yellow-tail is a very handsome fish about six inches long, chiefly sought for as bait, but making a capital fry in the absence of larger prey. Many other varieties of fish may be captured with a rod and line, among which are mullet, whiting, bream, rock-cod, sweeps (a

flattish black fish, of excellent flavor,) trum-
peters) a small striped fish, also well worth
the trouble of frying) ; and, in short, smaller
individuals of nearly all the kinds caught in
the deeper waters.

We hold, then, that a rod of somewhat better
description than the rude wands before mentioned, and a small assortment of tackle to be
used with it, are essential parts of a sportsman's equipment here as well as in England.
But this tackle may be of the cheapest description—strength only is necessary. The fish of
Port Jackson are bold biters, and are not to be
deterred by the use of even the coarsest tackle.
A common hazel rod, with three or four joints,
which may generally be procured for a few
shillings; two lines of silk twist, (that is, a
hand line of this material cut in two), which
will cost eight-pence, two cork floats, which
will, together, cost eight-pence or a shilling
more, and about six pennyworth of hooks and
gut will suffice for this branch of the fisherman's stock-in-trade. A good assortment of
hooks, however, an extra line or two, and a
fair supply of gut, will be found advantageous.

The places to which the angler may resort
with the greatest chance of success are the
wharfs where the larger ships lie, and the
deep waters where the shores are of a rocky
character. Warm sunny days, when there is
but little wind, are the best ; and the fish bite
more readily in the mornings and evenings
than at mid-day.

The common error into which the Sydney angler usually falls is in using hooks of too large a size. A small hook, if it is a good one, will suffice in the hands of a quick angler for the capture of a good-sized fish; while at the the same time it brings up many of the lesser kinds, which, if a large hook is used, will feed away at the bait with perfect impunity. Many of these bite so mincingly that a hook like that used for gudgeon and minnow in England— No. 13, we believe—will be found the most useful; with such a hook, a well-balanced float, and a tolerably quick eye and hand, few fish that approach the bait will escape capture.

The hand line, as we have already said, is the most common resource of Sydney fishermen, not only in boat fishing, but in fishing from the shore. In the latter case it is usually cast as far out as practicable into deep water, and a heavy leaden sinker is necessary not only for the purpose of bringing down the line itself, but in order to aid the operation of throwing it out. Larger fish are usually taken in this way than would be captured by rod fishing, but a true lover of the angle will always prefer the latter mode, and, with a skilful hand, it is far the most productive upon the whole.

But it is by fishing from a boat that the largest amount of sport may be ensured, and hence this kind of fishing is the only one which is ordinarily much cared for. The lines com-

monly used are those known in Sydney as
bream lines and schnapper lines - about thirty
fathoms long. A bream line may be procured at any of the ironmongers for a shilling, and a schnapper line for half-a-crown.
Hooks are equally cheap. In this kind of
fishing, as well as in fishing with a rod, it is
inadvisable to use large sized hooks, but experience is, upon this point, as upon most
others, the safest and best guide. It is unnecessary to use gut, except when fishing for
black bream, and as these are powerful fish it
is best that the gut should either be very
strong, or that a plait of two or three pieces
should be resorted to. It is generally advisable to use two or three hooks of various sizes,
the largest on the bottom, and the others at
short distances above.

A piece of fish is the best bait for most of the
kinds, but rock cod, bream, and many other
varieties, will seize as readily upon a piece of
fresh beef. The flesh of the yellow tail is
esteemed the most attractive and killing bait,
but we do not believe that there is much
squeamishness upon this point among the
dwellers in the waters. Muscles are an excellent bait for black bream, and for the perch of
the rivers there is nothing better than the common earth worm.

Night lines are laid with great success in the
rivers and lagoons. Cray-fish are captured in
baskets, and in shallow places the seine may
be always hauled with the certainty of pro-

curing a plentiful supply. A net of a peculiar construction, for deep waters, was used here by the crew of the *Ferrolana*, a Spanish vessel of war, with astonishing success, and was the means of bringing to the light several varieties of fish never before known to inhabit these waters. A model of this net has been taken, with a view to the manufacture of others of the same kind.

All the sea fish, and particularly the mullet, are excellent when salted and smoked, but this system of curing them has been but little resorted to. A Mr. Wilson had an establishment, some time since, for the sale of fish generally, in which the preparation and sale of cured fish was a prominent feature; but we regret to say that he did not meet with sufficient encouragement to continue his enterprise. The fact is, that the people of Sydney can buy fish so readily and so cheaply at their own doors from the men who hawk them about in wheelbarrows, that they will not, as yet, patronise a regular fishmonger's establishment to such an extent as to remunerate the proprietor for his outlay. A wide field for employment, however, lies untouched in this direction, whenever the pressure of circumstances and the wants of an increased population shall create a sufficient demand for food of the description alluded to.

By dwellers on or near the coast fish of all kinds are so readily procured as to be but little esteemed, and they are often greatly wasted.

Such persons, however, would do well to salt and cure their surplus fish. The process is a very simple one : gut and bone the fish, soak it for a short time in pickle, and smoke it either by the ordinary wood fire of the house, or in a small and close smoking hut of bark which may be put up for the purpose.

Sound practical knowledge in the fisherman's craft can only be acquired by experience, or by the example and instructions of those who have acquired this experience ; but the finny prey are here so abundant and are such ready feeders that no great skill is necessary in order to ensnare them, and those who attach themselves particularly to this branch of sport will readily afford to a new beginner the necessary information.

The smaller fish eat best fried or stewed, but the larger kinds are finest when baked. A rock cod of seven or eight pounds' weight, stuffed with green herbs, &c., well seasoned, well buttered, and served up with a sauce in which some good claret has been mixed to impart a flavor, furnishes a dish off which "the gods might dine." On fishing excursions, where a frying pan or a gridiron is not at hand, the best mode of cooking fish is that practised by savages— running a stick through the whole length of the body, and fixing this in the ground near the fire, turning it until the fish is done. Fish fresh taken and cooked in this way are delicious.

LEECHES.

Leeches are so plentiful in the swamps and water holes, and even in damp brush lands, as to be a pest. They may be captured readily by casting into the water the skin of a sheep or other animal recently killed, to the inner side of which they will attach themselves.

INDIGENOUS TIMBER.

No country on earth is better supplied with timber than Australia. Immense forests of stately eucalypti, and even in some districts of the more valuable cedar, are utterly worthless under present circumstances for want of a practicable route, either by land or water, to the market; or, at least, of such facilities of transport as might be taken advantage of without swallowing up the profits of the timber merchant.

There are few woods, however, that are of value for mere ornamental purposes, and the CEDAR (*Cedrela Australis*) is the only one of these worthy of particular mention; this however is a truly valuable timber. There are few varieties which have a more beautiful grain, or which, from their texture, are so well fitted for the purposes of the cabinet maker. The large size of the tree renders it equally valuable for building purposes, although the hard woods are more generally used. The cedar is found only in New South Wales in the vicinity of the coast ; on the banks of rivers and creeks, in gullies, and in the ravines of the coast ranges. The cedar forests accessible by water carriage have been so much thinned that the price has greatly increased of late years, and it has become a matter of dispute among the practical botanists of this colony as to whether the time has not arrived when cedar must be planted, and that extensively, in order to prevent a total failure of the supply at no very distant period.

Of the GUM *(Eucalyptus)* there are very many varieties, and some of them are exceedingly valuable for house and ship building. The Iron Bark, a dark, heavy, and hard wood, is the most durable of all the colonial timber ; in fact its durability is such, that the age of the colony has not permitted it to be as yet fairly tested. It is consequently much in demand, but owing to the difficulty of working it, it is dearer than the ordinary woods. It is exported to China and to Europe, for girders, being peculiarly fitted for this purpose. The aborigines prefer it to all other woods for their weapons, owing to its great weight and hardness. The blue and flooded gums are the woods chiefly used for ship and boat building. Black Butt, which grows to a great height and with remarkable straightness, is well adapted for masts, and is also greatly in demand for joists, rafters, flooring boards, &c. Stringy Bark is an equally valuable and useful timber. The bark of this variety being easily stripped from the tree, is much used for the roofs and even for the walls of the shepherds' huts. Many trees, in fact, are destroyed by stripping off circles of bark for this purpose. There are many other trees of the gum family, all more or less used for building or for fencing.

The PINES, although some of them are of surpassing beauty, are not peculiarly valuable as timber trees. The Moreton Bay pine is sometimes used for spars, but it is not well adapted for this purpose, being much too brittle. It is light however, and easily wrought, and is consequently preferred for packing cases, and other light works of a similar nature. Excellent canoes are made by the aborigines from its bark. It is very plentiful on and near the north-east coast, but has not been found to the southward of the Clarence River. The Bunya Bunya is a fine handsome tree, the tallest in fact in New Holland, found only in the vicinity of Moreton Bay. Its name signifies in the native dialect, a very large tree ; twice tree, or tree-tree. Its timber is believed to be good, but as its seed forms at certain seasons the chief food of the aborigines, a sort of embargo has been placed upon it by the Colonial Government.

Various species of the *Casuarina*, which is here termed the OAK, although very different in its aspect from the monarch of the English forest, are found throughout the colony. It is a tough grained and reddish colored wood, and is much used for shingles, sheep hurdles, staves, &c. A tree of a different species to these, but known as the SILVER OAK, (*Grevillea robusta*) is very valuable to coopers as furnishing the finest stave timber. It is found only to the northward of the Hunter.

The AUSTRALIAN BEECH (*Monotoca elliptica*) yields a hard wood which is used for mallets and other tools, in fact for all the purposes to which the wood of the English beech is applied. It is found near the coast in all parts of this colony. The MANGROVE, which is found in the immediate vicinity of the salt water, yields a tough wood, which makes excellent blocks, and is used by shipwrights for that purpose. Its crooked limbs are also found exceedingly useful for boats' knees. The ashes of the mangrove were formerly much used in the manufacture of soap, but they have been superseded by soda.

To the timber trade in its various branches we shall have occasion to refer in a subsequent part of our work.

NATIVE FRUITS.

The wild fruits are neither very numerous nor very rich. The seed of the BUNYA BUNYA pine, already mentioned, merits the first place, owing to its great usefulness to the aborigines as a staple article of food. The cones of this tree are large, and the seed resembles a nut in character and taste. The NATIVE CURRANT, a small green berry growing thickly upon a low sized shrub, very commonly met with in the neighbourhood of Sydney, has an agreeable acid taste, and is much used by the colonists to make jams and jellies of. The latter are delicious : made thick, cut in squares, and used with cream, native current jelly is no bad substitute for strawberries. It is probable that this plant might be much improved by cultivation.

The NATIVE RASPBERRY resembles the common raspberry of Europe, but is very inferior to it in flavour. The CAPE GOOSEBERRY differs in appearance only from the common gooseberry by having a sheath round the fruit. Both are common. The QUONDONG, found to the westward of our cordillera, is a fruit about the size of a peach, which is used by the settlers for puddings and pies, and sometimes, although rarely, raw. It is eaten by the emu, and the stones, which are about the size of a marble, are collected by the natives after they have been voided by that bird, in order that they may be used for tobacco. They are prepared for the pipe by pounding. The cone of the ENAM or SCREW PINE, which resembles a pine-apple, is greedily eaten by the natives after having undergone a slight fermentation. It has a sweet flavor, resembling that of honey. but is very fibrous, and sticks most unpleasantly to the teeth. The ILLAWARRA PLUM (one of the *Podocarpi*) is a large and well flavored fruit, resembling the plums of Europe. The AUS-

TRALIAN TAMARIND is a tall tree, growing in nearly all the scrubs and jungles near the coast, and bearing a fruit resembling in appearance and taste the tamarind of the West Indies. Some of the larger species of a plant called by the colonists PIG-FACE (*Mesembryanthemum,*) bear a fruit not unlike a fig. These plants are exceedingly plentiful in barren grounds near the coast, and besides yielding the fruit just alluded to, they are valuable for two other purposes: they bear an elegant flower, and their stems and leaves are excellent for pickling.

The MORETON BAY CHESNUT, a very beautiful and stately tree, bears a fruit which, although almost poisonous to an European, is eaten by the blacks without injury, after they have by pounding and by careful preparation deprived it of its acrid and unwholesome juice. The seed of the common AUSTRALIAN PALM, (*Zamia Spiralis*) which grows in a large green cone resembling a pine apple, is also prepared and eaten in a similar manner.

There are several berries eaten both by the natives and the children of the settlers, geebungs, five-corners, lillia-pillias, &c.; none of these, however, are of any value either for flavour or as affording nutricious food.

INDIGENOUS TREES, &c., GENERALLY.

The CABBAGE TREE (*Corypha*), although it frequently attains a great height, yields no timber suitable for ordinary building purposes. For the erection of such primitive structures as are found sufficient for most purposes in the bush, it is, however, very useful. The trunk splits with great ease, and yields slabs with a surface much smoother than the more heavy and enduring timber of the Eucalypti. The cabbage tree slabs, however, do not last very long, and in order to preserve them more effectually, it is necessary that their lower extremities should be raised clear of the earth, either by means of a stone foundation or of wooden sleepers. The common name of the tree has been derived from its yielding an edible substance, similar in flavor to a cabbage. This substance is the imperfectly formed central bud, and in order to procure it the destruction of the whole tree is necessary. To obtain this "cabbage," and to procure materials for making hats, an immense number of these beautiful and stately palms are destroyed annually. The part used for hat making is the young central leaves. These undergo a process of steeping and bleaching, after which they are twisted, or rather plaited, into what is termed "sennet", and then made up into low-crowned broad-brimmed hats, shaped and finished according to the taste and skill of the manufacturer. This branch of industry is not practised as a trade, but is followed by hut-keepers and other bushmen, who having some leisure time on their hands, resort to this expedient for increasing their income. The cabbage tree hats are handsome and durable, and are consequently much used. By the native youth, in fact, they are regarded as a sort of national badge.

The ACACIAS are numerous in the extreme, and are all very beautiful, although none of them attain the rank of timber trees. The most common kinds are those known among the colonists as WATTLES, (green wattle and black wattle). Owing to the rapid growth of these trees, as well as to their beauty, they are much esteemed for ornamental purposes. A whole grove may be raised in a couple of years, but they do not last long, and it is therefore necessary that a young growth should be planted in readiness to succeed the older trees as they die off, or are cut away for firewood. The bark of these trees is astringent, some of it particularly so, and it is very useful for tanning purposes. A strong decoction of wattle bark, carefully used, has been found an effectual remedy in cases of dysentery. The gum which exudes from the stems of these trees in great abundance, is clear, sweet, and transparent. When fresh it is frequently gathered by the natives for food, and when dry resembles in appearance and properties the well known gum arabic of commerce.

The GRASS TREE is not, properly speaking, a tree at all. From out of an immense and spreading tuft of long, tough, and grass-like leaves, springs a long slender shaft like a bulrush. This, when dry, is peculiarly light,

M

although hard in texture, and from the readiness with which it ignites by friction it is much used by the natives as a means of obtaining fire. From among the old leaves and roots of the grass tree is procured an abundance of gum, exactly resembling gamboge in its color and general appearance. This gum has an agreeable although strongly medicinal odour, especially when burnt. It is powerfully astringent, and has been found an effective medicine in cases of dysentery, but requires to be used with great care.

All the eucalypti produce gum resin in abundance, and much of this has been exported—although it has not, we believe, been found very valuable. Sometimes, however, it has been put to a less worthy purpose on the spot. The writer of this paper once saw, in company with several others, a full cask of gum, drawn from a comparatively small tree near Canterbury, (a village on the banks of Cook's river, about seven miles from Sydney), which was procured for the adulteration of Colonial ale.

The WARATAH, or native tulip, which bears a magnificent scarlet blossom, is used for all the purposes to which osiers are applied in England. A small shrub with silky seed pods, called by the colonists the COTTON TREE is equally useful for the same purpose. The down to which the seeds of the latter plant are attached makes superb pillows, but is not, we believe, durable.

There are wild plants having the properties

of FLAX, and some of them are called by that name. They are not, however, of any material use. There has indeed been some discussion as to whether one plant of this description might not be cultivated with advantage; but as it resembles the New Zealand flax (*Phormium tenax*), and as the latter, which is of superior fineness, could be produced with equal facility, it is to this that the growers will most naturally turn their attention, whenever the work of flax culture shall be seriously entered upon.

There are many varieties of EDIBLE ROOTS in the Australian bush, but they are known to few beside the aborigines. Of these, a tuberous root, known as the native yam, is the principal. Some of the fern roots afford passable food, and even among the grasses there are varities which contribute in this way to the subsistence of the wandering tribes of Australia.

There are several plants used by bushmen as substitutes for tea. The principal of these is a creeper bearing a black berry, a blue flower, and a long green leaf, abundant in the neighbourhood of the metropolis, which, from its being used in this way, is known as SWEET TEA by the colonists. In flavour it somewhat reresembles liquorice, and like the latter, is esteemed a valuable medicine for coughs.

INDIGO is abundant in a wild state, but no attempt at indigo planting, as a work of commercial enterprise, has yet been made. Useful and valuable dye woods also exist, but the knowledge of them is chiefly confined to the few persons who have had occasion to experimentalise upon them for manufacturing purposes. From a large species of wild vine, which grows plentifully on the banks of the northern rivers, known to the aborigines as curranbilly, and to the settlers as cockspur, Mr. Gee, of Sydney, has produced a beautiful yellow. By the use of the "mordaunt," and other means of varying colors known to dyers, Mr. Gee has produced all shades of this color, from a pale golden tint to a deep yellowish brown. All the shades are good and durable; the dyed wools having been well tested to be certain of the latter fact. The wood itself is very handsome, of a deep brownish yellow, with fine veins of a lighter color, and of satin like appearance when polished. It works well, especially in the lathe, and would prove valuable to the turner and the cabinet-maker. It is the inner part of the stems alone that has been used to prepare the dye, and it has been found to yield about twenty-five per cent. more of coloring matter, and that of a better quality, than can be obtained from fustic. And yet it is much more economical than the latter, even if it were only of equal usefulness, for while fustic costs £12 per ton, this colonial wood could be brought into the Sydney Market for £5 per ton at the outside.

The wild GRASSES, although, as might be expected, not so close in their growth as the green clothing of the English meadows, afford excellent food to the immense flocks and herds which are scattered throughout the districts beyond the boundaries of location, and of which we shall have to speak more fully when we come to treat of pastoral occupations.

There are doubtless many other productions, valuable for human sustenance, for medicinal purposes, or for commerce, among the indigenous trees, plants, and herbage of Australia. But although our country affords a wider scope for the labours of the Botanist than any other land on the earth's surface, and although in fact, we have scientific gentlemen among us, by whom extensive acquaintance with this division of nature's gifts has been acquired, there has not as yet been any publication, on the spot, of information so much needed. We trust that no lengthened period will elapse before this great want is supplied.

To comment upon the immense variety, and surpassing beauty, of the Australian wild flowers would be foreign to our purpose. And even if it were not so, no mere description could convey to the distant reader a just idea of the reality. Suffice it to say, that many plants which in England are highly prized tenants of the conservatory and the hot house, are in Australia as abundant as mere weeds.

BUSHCRAFT.

The wilds of Australia being designated, in colonial parlance, " the Bush," we use the term Bushcraft as an appropriate one for that knowledge of the wilderness and its ways which is elsewhere cal ed Woodcraft.

This knowledge is a most essential branch of a colonist's training, if he seeks to penetrate the interior ; yet it can only be acquired by experience. But with fair powers of observation, and a readiness to acquire and retain informa-, tion from whatever quarter it may be procurable, the immigrant may soon become a tolerable bushman. Among his older fellow-colonists he will find the disposition as well as the ability to guide and instruct him.

Within the settled districts travelling is a very simple matter. The highways, although often, perhaps usually, in bad order, are so well defined that it is difficult even for a stranger to miss his way ; unless he is deluded into taking "a short cut through the bush," in the vain hope of arriving with greater speed and less bodily exertion at some given point, instead of adhering to the main road. This, by the by, is the way in which most persons, even old bushmen, get bewildered. No inexperienced hand should ever trust himself to the chances of safely traversing these " short cuts," for although they often save a good deal of time and distance to those who are thoroughly acquainted with them, they are just as often a source of delay and trouble to those of the inexperienced who seek by their aid to lessen their own fatigues. And yet the temptation is often very strong.

The "old hands," who are acquainted with these by-paths, are ever ready to point them out to the wayfarer, and, estimating his perceptive faculties by the erroneous standard of their own experience they will usually assure him that " it is impossible he can miss his way." The traveller seldom gets far before he discovers that it is barely possible for him to *find* his way. Paths dwindle to mere tracks, branching off, perhaps, in all directions, and amidst the natural objects which surround him he finds a degree of uniformity sufficient to baffle every attempt to make out the particular landmarks which he may have been instructed to seek. A person who finds himself in this position will take the wisest course, if he makes the best of his way back to the high road.

Along the highways which traverse the settled districts, there are almost everywhere good inns sufficiently near each other to be within reach even of the pedestrian. And the excellence of the country inns, in particular, is a matter of surprise to the inexperienced traveller, who thinks he has left all of luxury, if not of comfort, behind in the metropolis. In most places he will find the accommodation good, the fare superior, and the charges, upon the whole, moderate.

Travelling by the mail is the most common mode of journeying among young colonists. This is a very different thing from travelling by the old mails and stage

coaches in England. Although the
journeys here are performed with comparative
rapidity, when the nature of the country and
the state of the roads are taken into consideration, there is none of that extreme hurry with
which we have been tormented on the English
roads. There is no tearing away of the half-
famished traveller from his scarcely tasted
meal. Time is allowed him to feed heartily,
before the coachman summonses him to resume
his place. But there are many other peculiarities of Australian mail-coach travelling,
some of which are, in the opinion of many,
not quite so agreeable.

The coaches which come into Sydney are
usually handsome and commodious vehicles ;
but before many stages from the metropolis
are got over, the traveller finds himself packed
in a sort of oblong box, open to the elements,
licensed to carry at least fifty per cent. more of
passengers and luggage than it will conveniently hold. A few jolts, however—and many
pretty severe ones may be calculated upon—
soon shake every one into position ; and, as the
driver is usually both skilful and obliging,
things pass on pretty well. When a steep
hill, or any other impediment of a similar
nature, tehnically termed a " pinch," has to be
encountered, the coachman requests his male
passengers to alight, and " walk on a bit."
Some of these walks extend upwards of a mile,
but after being packed up in a Western or
Southern mail, like herrings in a barrel, this

exercise is found a relief rather than otherwise, especially if the weather is fine.

Practised bushmen usually travel on horseback, or with drays, according to their means and exigencies ; and where a new hand has an opportunity of traversing the country under guidance such as men of this stamp can afford him, he will act wisely in availing himself of it. An equestrian thoroughly acquainted with the country, seldom fails, even in the wildest region, to make out a halting place where he can find bush fare, a hearty welcome, and a good night's rest, beneath the shelter of a roof. Travelling with a dray has more of the romantic in it than a stranger would imagine. Drays seldom go singly, but in parties, halting each night at a convenient camping place. The draymen and their fellow-travellers make a temporary hut beneath the vehicles, where they rest soundly, their dogs keeping a vigilant watch around the camp fires. Some of these encampments seen at nightfall or at early dawn, have a very picturesque appearance.

There is something very attractive in the free and healthful life of the bushman. Few that have acquired a taste for this kind of life can ever be contented or happy in the towns. And such a taste is acquired by the majority of those who have resided for any length of time in the interior.

A bush life is not necessarily one of hardship and privation. Stately edifices, indeed,

are unknown in the wilds, but many of the
farmers, and even of the squatters, have surrounded themselves not only with comforts,
but with luxuries.   Their houses are often
commodious, their gardens large, and well
stocked, and their dairies well managed, while
at the same time, they have an abundance of
fowls, &c., ready at hand whenever they are
wanted.   With these conveniences, and with
a regular supply of wines, groceries, and other
luxuries, received through the intervention of
the carriers, the bushman who is well to do in
the world, gets on admirably.   These social
improvements are usually most manifest
where the settler is himself "settled"—that is,
when he has a wife and family to share his
home.   Many of the bachelor squatters are
still incorrigible in their adherence to bark
huts, black pipes, salt beef, and damper.

Luxuries such as those above mentioned
are of course beyond the reach of the shepherd
and the stockman, but even the labouring
classes do not fare badly in the bush.   Salt
meat, tea, and damper (an unleavened loaf
baked in the hot ashes,) form their staple food,
and their huts are usually not only
weather proof, but comfortable.   The
presence of women has, with the men as
with the masters, done most towards softening down the barbarism which, until lately,
prevailed in the unsettled districts.

But on the frontiers, and throughout the
almost trackless wilds of the far interior,

where even the stations of the squatters are but widely scattered, the life of the bushman is still one of adventure and of peril. His habitation, his clothing, and his fare are of the most simple kind. In traversing the country around him he has no guide but his personal knowledge of its features, and his experience in bush-travelling. He has constantly to guard against the inroads of the aborigines, who, although they usually content themselves with preying upon his sheep and cattle, will occasionally attack himself with a view of getting possession of his stores. Many and many a collision takes place between these pioneers of colonisation and the sable lords of the wild, of which not even the slightest rumour ever reaches Sydney.

But the life of the bushman has been graphically described by most of those who have laid before the public narratives of their sojourn and wanderings in Australia, and to these narratives we must refer our readers for those details of bush scenery and adventures which it would be foreign to our purpose to enter upon.

A knowledge of bushcraft is not more necessary to any class of persons, than to sportsmen. The sportsman can never pursue his most attractive amusements with pleasure and with safety until he has acquired this knowledge. The pursuit of game will generally lead him into wild and densely timbered tracts from whence nothing but practical

knowledge or a fortunate accident can extri-
cate him. And with all his knowledge and
care, he may often have to camp out for the
night. He should never, therefore, be un-
provided for such a contingency,

So many persons " go out a shooting" from
Sydney, without taking any of the necessary
precautions or making any of the necessary
provisions for being lost in the bush, that it
is a matter of surprise they do not pay more
often and more severely for their temerity.
But the fact is they seldom do more than
ramble near the beaten paths of the suburbs,
and as a natural consequence they generally
do but little towards filling their game bags.

In the first place no man should start out to
traverse the scrubs, as a sportsman ought to
do, without putting on a pair of stoutish boots,
and providing himself with leggings of leather
or fustian, so as to resist a snake bite. Most
persons who have been bitten would have
come off scathless if they had adopted this
precaution, and the few who have been wise
enough to do so, can tell of repeated escapes in
consequence. There are five other things
which he should never be without a pocket
compass, a large strong made clasp knife, a
small vessel to drink from, a piece of sponge,
and the means of making a fire. The usefulness of the first three articles is obvious. The
sponge may be the means of saving him from
the torments of unsatisfied thirst, in the event
of his being benighted in a place where there

is no water near. During most nights there is a considerable dew, and by the aid of a sponge a comparative abundance of moisture may be collected from the grass and foliage, although without its aid no such supply could be procured. For making a fire nothing beats our old friend the tinder-box. Lucifer matches, although first-rate articles at home, are often from dam_ or from wind utterly useless in the bush. Small tinder-boxes suitable for this kind of service may be purchased cheaply in Sydney, and a sort of fungus which grows upon dead timber, and is well known to most colonists by the name of " punk," makes, when scorched, the best tinder. The ordinary German tinder, however, is very good. By its aid a few pieces of dry bark may be lighted, and with the addition of a twig or two and some dry leaves, there is speedily sufficient foundation to " build," as the phrase is, a large fire. The blacks procure fire very readily by means of the grass tree, but few whites succeed in doing this, until they have seen it practised several times by their sable brethren. The best mode is this. Cut a piece of the dried stalk of the grass tree in two ; point one half, and hollow out in a cup shape one end of the other half, so that the pointed part may fit as nearly as possible the hollowed part ; put the hollowed piece between the knees and inserting the point of the other, which is held between the palms of the hands, twirl it rapidly and regularly round by moving the

N

hands backwards and forwards. If this is dexterously managed the friction will soon produce fire.

Want of water is the evil which he who traverses the bush has most to fear. In some parts of the country, rivulets and water-holes are only to be met with at remote distances from each other: in the scrubby lands intersected by deep gullies, or ravines such lands as the sportsman would naturally most resort to — a small brook or a piece of swampy ground will usually be found at the lowest point of each gully. Towards night-fall such places may be traced out by the croaking of the frogs. During the day the approach to a river or to any considerable sheet of water may be known by observing the flight of the cormorants and other aquatic birds. But in the wilds, the chances of having to camp without water are so great, that the sponge is, as we have before mentioned, a part of the sportsman's equipment that ought never to be forgotten.

Sportsmen and travellers are often lost almost beyond redemption by trying to extricate themselves from their difficulties after darkness has fairly set in upon them. By so doing they are almost certain to get deeper into the wilds, and to lose all the traces by which they might hope to return as they came. The best and the safest course when a wayfarer in the bush finds that night will certainly overtake him before he can retrace his steps or complete his journey onward, is for him to stop for the night at the first eligible spot that presents itself. The vicinity of water is the most important thing. Where water is fou d, a sheltered spot can almost invariably be pitched upon close at hand, and a few bushes rapidly torn down and interlaced to windward of the place where the wayfarer intends to rest, will, in an Australian climate, answer every purpose unless the weather be unpropitious. Fern, small branches, or bushes, will make an excellent couch if the ground be damp; and indeed, under any circumstances, it is advisable to strew a few of these on the spot selected as a sleeping-place.

A party of three or four may "camp out" with much greater comfort than a single individual. Consequently, when sportsmen plunge into the wilds in search of game they should go in such parties, or at all events in couples. If they set out with the determination of passing a night or two in the bush, each person should carry a blanket or rug. One should also carry a small vessel to make tea with, and another a light hatchet or tomahawk. By the aid of the latter a sufficient quantity of bushes for shelter and repose may speedily be cut down. If a natural cover of trees and shrubs presents itself so much the better, and in most cases a place may readily be found where, with but little labour, a well sheltered camp may be formed. At a short distance, and in the direction towards which the feet of the sleepers will be pointed when they retire to rest, the fire should be made, care being taken to remove from its vicinity all dry grass, leaves, or twigs, which might ignite and carry the flame into the surrounding bush. If damp weather should set in and a perfectly sheltered spot cannot be found to camp in, one or more blankets, according to the number of the party, should be strained in the form of a roof, while bushes are piled up on either side for walls, sufficiently high to allow of the party sitting upright within. With such precautions, with a good fire, and with good bush fare, the sportsman may defy the weather.

There are still many places within a day's journey of the metropolis to which sporting parties might resort at the proper season with much profit and amusement, although the larger game has for the most part been driven off to regions farther removed. The best mode of proceeding is this. The party should start for their proposed hunting ground at such an hour as to arrive there in the afternoon. A camping place should then be selected, and a shelter constructed. Here the party may rest for the night, and here also they may muster on the following day for the purposes of refreshment, and for comparing their good or ill fortune as hunters. For this reason the camp should be in a central position, and on a slight elevation ; near it a fire should be kept up. The smoke, during the day, or after nightfall the fire itself, would serve as a guide to the spot; but each person should nevertheless take bearings carefully before quitting the camp. Three days, one in going to the ground, a second for actual sport, and a third for the return, may in fine weather be thus very pleasantly and healthfully spent.

In the far interior the traveller looks out for a station, and there are many indications by which the approach to one is at once made known to a practised eye. The excrement of cattle, the marks of the axe where wood has been cut for burning, or bark removed for hut-building; and, on a nearer approach, the barking of dogs, and the note of chanticleer, are among these indications.

The way from one place to another in the interior is often pointed out by lines of marked trees only. In such a case the utmost vigilance is necessary, for the line is easily lost, and difficult to find again; and it is usually across a heavy and wild country that those lines are carried. Many such lines are formed for the sake of shortening the distance between two points even when there is a practicable and well beaten but more circuitous road. In such cases the traveller who is not versed in bushcraft will usually find it most to his advantage to keep on the highway.

Equestrians should always carry hobbles for their horses. To hobble the horses while their riders bivouac in the bush is generally better than tethering them, especially in scrubby lands; and if both horses and cattle have been accustomed to carry bells, so that they may be traced by the sound, it will be all the better, for much time is often lost in the morning in hunting up the animals before making a start.

When a party of sportsmen, instead of forming a particular camp as a resting-place during the whole time of their excursion, shall deem it better to proceed separately towards a more distant place of rendezvous, the position and bearings of this place should be distinctly understood, and if it is deep in the bush he who arrives there first should at once make a fire to guide the rest.

As a general rule it will be found well to secure, if practicable, the presence and assistance of an aboriginal native with all such parties. The aid of one or more of these can in most cases be obtained for a trifling consideration; and their sagacity in finding game, in searching out water, or in tracking any of the party who may happen to miss his way, renders them well worthy of their hire. No intoxicating drink, however, should be given to them, and it is better, indeed, that nothing of this kind should form a part of the equipment.

PART II.

WHALES AND WHALING.

THROUGHOUT the vast Pacific, which washes the shores of the Australian Continent, the sperm whale is hunted and destroyed by adventurous seamen of all nations. Many of the vessels engaged in this fishery belong to Sydney Houses, and the export of Oil and other whaler's produce to Europe is very considerable, to say nothing of its consumption in the colony itself.

Although great attention has been directed to the sperm whale by scientific men, it would still seem that there is much to learn, not only as to the habits of these animals, but as to the number of varieties included in the family to which they belong. There is much reason to believe that Sydney will be the scene of the most important investigations into this subject, and of the discoveries by which these investigations will doubtless be rewarded. Already we have promise of this. Two skeletons have been set up at the Sydney Museum by Mr. Wall, the Curator, who has published a most able and interesting work upon this subject, describing these skeletons anatomically, and demonstrat-

o

ing the existence of a new genus of sperm whales, called *Euphysetes.* The work of investigation thus entered on will doubtless be followed up. Much valuable information and aid may be expected from the captains of whaling vessels, the attention of many of them having been called to the subject ; and we have among our colonists naturalists of high standing, who will not fail to take advantage of all such information as can be attained.

The SPERM WHALE is one of that division of animals termed " Cetacea," which includes also many other species destroyed by man for the sake of the oil which they yield. Some of these we shall have hereafter to speak of.

This monster of the deep is, when full grown, about eighty feet long, with a circumference of from thirty to thirty-five feet. The head is abrupt or blunted at the extremity, clumsy in appearance, and generally about one third of the entire length of the animal. The mouth is enormous, extending the whole length of the head, but the lower jaw only is furnished with teeth, which though formidable enough in appearance, are, considering the vast size of the animal, far too small for the purposes of mastication. The whales, therefore, consume their food without this preparatory process. The tongue is small, but the gullet is large enough to take in the body of a man. Nothing, however, which is larger than a medium sized fish ever passes that way. The mouth is lined throughout with a pearly white membrane, and it is asserted that the glistening of this membrane is of service to the animal in its feeding, by attracting the " squids" and small fish upon which it feeds ; the whale poising itself vertically in the water, with its mouth open, for this purpose, until a supply of the unlucky animals have been seduced within the vortex. The squid is a kind of cuttle fish, which forms the staple of the sperm whale's diet. The skin of the whale is dark, varying in shade according to its age. In young whales the skin is about three-eighths of an inch thick, but as the creature grows older it diminishes in thickness, until it is as thin as one-eighth.

Immediately beneath the skin lies the blubber or fat, which, in a full grown whale, varies from eight to fourteen inches in depth. It is of a light yellow colour, and furnishes, when melted, the sperm oil of commerce; upwards of eighty barrels being often procured from a full grown male. It is called by seamen the " blanket ;" and has, indeed, the effect of a blanket in protecting the animal from the cold of the surrounding waters. In the head is a large and almost triangular cavity, called by whalers, the " case," wherein is secreted an oily liquor, which after death hardens into a yellowish granulated substance—the spermaceti of commerce. From the head of a large whale upwards of a tun, or ten barrels, of spermaceti is frequently procurable.

The sperm whale makes its way through the

water by the aid of its tail, or "flukes," but it is provided with two swimming paws, wherewith it can guide itself, and with which, as with hands, the female is said to clasp her young to her breast.

Whalemen speak of these animals as herdsmen do of their cattle. The males are termed bulls; the females, cows; the young ones, calves. A number of whales however is not termed a herd, but a school. The females, which are much smaller than the males, are found associated together in these schools, and with them are generally two or three sturdy bulls, who are designated by sailors as schoolmasters. These partiarchal gentlemen are said to resent most fiercely the approach of any interlopers of their own sex and species. The male calves also go in schools. The old bulls, however, are generally found singly, and while from their bulk they are the most profitable to the whaler, they are easier to kill than the females, bearing the strokes of the harpoon and the lance with more patience and using less strenuous efforts to escape. But it is only the *old* bulls which are thus so apparently resigned to their fate. The young bulls are exceedingly wary, and are very difficult to capture. Those yielding about forty barrels, and called forty-barrel bulls, by the whalemen, are the most troublesome. Occasionally, the whales make a violent resistance, staving the boats and doing all manner of mischief; but more usually, all their efforts are directed towards escape. Their timidity is fortunate, for an animal of such enormous bulk as the sperm whale would otherwise be a terrible foe, under any circumstances.

The females display much care and affection for their young, and the cow is often killed while aiding her calf to escape. In like manner, the young animals will frequently remain near the spot where their parents have been deprived of life. The females will also hover round, or " heave to," as the sailors have it, when one of their number is wounded. Thus, a whole school has sometimes been destroyed by bold and skilful fishers. It is different, however, with a school of young bulls. No sooner is one of them wounded than the rest take the alarm and make off in all directions, leaving their comrade to his fate. It is a singular fact that all sperm whales have some means of communicating to each other, even when far apart, the approach of danger. What these means are has not been ascertained, but the fact itself is undeniable.

The sperm whale being, in common with all the rest of the cetacea, a warm blooded and respiring animal, is compelled to rise to the surface of the water in order to breathe. This it does at regular intervals, and its motions in this respect are so precise that experienced whalemen can calculate with certainty the time of the whale's sinking below the surface. It is by the vapour and water which is spouted forth from the nostrils of the whale when it rises for the purpose of respiration that its presence is made known to the look-out men stationed at the mast-head of the whaling vessels. They are seen in this way at a distance of several miles. When alarmed the sperm whale indulges in many antics, very different from the ordinary regularity of its movements, sweeping the surface of the water with its tail, and even placing itself in a perpendicular position, with the whole of its enormous head above water, in order that it may better command a view of surrounding objects. When a whale has thus taken the alarm, it is said by the fisher to be " gallied," and great energy and caution is necessary on the part of its pursuers.

The black, or as the seamen term it, the RIGHT WHALE, is less sought for in the seas around Australia than the kind already spoken of. It is much smaller than the common black whale of the northern regions, measuring usually from thirty-five to forty feet in length, although occasionally met with as long as fifty feet. In colour and general appearance, however, it closely resembles its northern prototype, so much so that they were at one time believed to be of the same species. The oil of this animal is very inferior in quality to that procured from the sperm whale, but on the other hand, it is from the black kind that the well-known whalebone of commerce is procured. This substance is taken from the mouth, where it serves the animal as a substitute for teeth. As much as a ton of this whalebone, or baleen, as it is more properly called, is often obtained from a full grown black whale of the northern species. The whales of the south are less productive on account of their diminished size, but the quantity of baleen which is obtainable from them is greater in proportion to the entire bulk of the animal than that which is procurable from the northern variety.

There is a species of whale called by those engaged in the south sea fishery the BLACK-FISH or BLACK-WHALE, but known to the naturalist as the Southern Rorqual, which the whalemen usually avoid. Although a large animal, being frequently as long as forty feet, and proportionately bulky, this creature has less blubber than either of the kinds already mentioned, and the oil obtained from it is of an inferior description. It is besides so active and powerful that its capture is all but impossible.

There has been of late years a great falling off in the whaling operations of the Sydney merchants, as the statistics given in the appendix will show. This is to be deplored, and the more so because it is chiefly attributable to want of enterprise and skill on the part of those connected with the fishery. It is true that whaling cruises have not been so profitable of late, and when the wholesale manner in which these huge creatures have been hunted out and destroyed comes to be considered, it is scarcely surprising. But with skill, energy, and perseverance, the South Sea Fishery is still a money-making enterprise. The Americans, at all events, have contrived to make it so. All the seas around us are traversed by their whaling ships, which are usually fine and well furnished vessels, and are generally successful enough to afford their owners and crew a handsome return for the investment of the former and the enterprise of the latter. The position of New South Wales, of the neighbouring Australasian colonies, and of New Zealand, ought to give them, collectively, almost a mastery of the fishery; but the active and persevering mariners of the United States have decidedly obtained the upper hand in this fishery, as they have also in the very lucrative traffic with the almost innumerable islands of Polynesia. The establishment at the Auckland Islands for the purpose of prosecuting the southern fishery systematically, may do much; but this remains to be seen.

It is, we believe, to a want of scientific information on the part of those who are entrusted with the conduct of whaling operations—a want of knowledge as to the habits of the creatures they are in pursuit of, which has been the chief cause of failure. Whalers run hither and thither in search of their prey, and either meet with it or not as their good or evil stars may be in the ascendant; whereas a knowledge of the whale's habits, of its migrations, and of the seasons of those migrations, might enable them to proceed at once to the spot where the animals were to be taken. This knowledge is only to be acquired by observation, by a record of the facts observed, and by a scientific examination of these facts, so as to arrive at the proper conclusions to which they point. Suppose, for instance, that the stomach of the whale was invariably searched to ascertain the nature of its food at the time of its capture, and a record kept of the observations thus made. Suppose, as a next step, it could be ascertained in what places and at what times the particular kinds of food used by the whales were most plentiful. The result would show where and when whales might with certainty be met with. It is by observations such as these, that experienced whaling masters are enabled to ensure success. Now, although much interesting and useful information may *occasionally* be procured from the captains and officers of whaling vessels, it is but seldom that they are willing to communicate the result of their experience to others. And this reluctance is natural. It is the interest of the individual to keep his knowledge for his own benefit. But the interest of the community, and especially of a community so circumstanced as New South Wales, requires that a compilation of facts and deductions should be made for the benefit of all. This could only be done under the auspices of the Government, of the Legislature, or of the mercantile body, by setting one or more competent individuals to the task of investigation.

The Australian whalers are for the most part of from 200 to 300 tons burthen. All on board, from the captain downwards, are paid by a share of the oil procured, which share is called, in whalemen's parlance, a "lay," and is proportioned, of course, to the rank and ability of the man. The dangers and excitement of whaling have been frequently and most graphically sketched; but there is one feature of this trade in the Pacific, which is not so generally known. It is the intercourse of those who follow it with the interesting tribes of Polynesia. Whaling captains generally seek some of the islands for the purpose of procuring supplies of provisions, or of repairing slight damages sustained at sea, because, in the first place, they can obtain provisions there at infinitely less cost than in any of the colonial ports; and in the second place they find it easier by this course to keep their men together. Supplies are frequently, also, procured in boats, without bringing the vessel to an anchor. These supplies, consisting of pigs and fowls, with yams, cocoanuts, bread fruit, and other productions of a similar nature, are obtained by barter; calicoes, hardware, common trinkets, and other matters likely to be prized by the untutored Islanders being carried for that purpose. These articles are technically known as "trade." Among the native races the whalemen exercise a doubtful influence. From his English or American brother, the Polynesian learns something of the white man's science, but too often he learns far more of the white man's evil ways. All the precautions which the Captains can take is insufficient to prevent occasional desertion; and extraordinarily numerous as are the islands of the Pacific, there is scarcely one of them which has not one or more runaway sailors domesticated among the people who inhabit it.

The Eden-like features of these Islands, and the vast influence which even the most ignorant white man acquires among the Islanders, are attractions too powerful to be resisted. But the influence of the white man is usually exerted for evil rather than for good, for it is generally individuals of the worst class who are most ready to abandon their connection with civilised man, in order to lord it amongst savages.

Bay whaling, or the capture of whales by parties stationed on shore, who run off to the chase in boats whenever a whale heaves in sight, was formerly much practised. At present, we are not aware of its being carried on in any other place than Twofold Bay. The boats used in bay whaling are generally much larger and more strongly made than those attached to the vessels engaged in the Fishery.

Besides the oil and spermaceti, the valuable ambergris of commerce is procured from the sperm whale. It is found in the intestinal canal, but in uncertain quantities; frequently indeed, it is altogether wanting.

The bones of all the whales are too porous to be of much value; walking-sticks and other trifles are, however, occasionally made from them by the sailors, for which a good price is obtained. It is a matter of surprise that the least porous bones of the whale have not been used for this purpose by tradesmen. The teeth of the sperm whale, being much prized by the Polynesian islanders as ornaments, are usually bartered away for supplies. They are, however, used by colonial workmen as a substitute for ivory.

SEALS.

Seals are plentiful on some parts of the southern coast, and on the islands in its vicinity. Formerly vessels were often fitted out for the sole purpose of sealing, but the herds have been so much thinned and scattered by the reckless havoc which has been made among them that such expeditions are no longer profitable. The practice was to leave small parties of men at various stations where seals were to be met with, and to pick them up at a future period with such spoil as they had managed in the mean time to secure. Sealing is now followed almost exclusively, we believe, by a semi-barbarous set of men residing on the islands in Bass' Straits. These sealers are of three classes—runaway seamen, fugitives from penal settlements in the neighbourhood, or half-castes, the result of an union between the men of the two first-named classes with female aborigines carried off from the Australian main. By persons occupying this isolated position, and by residents on the coast near spots where seals are to be found in any numbers, the pursuit and capture of these animals will usually be found very profitable.

We are not able to state with accuracy what kinds of the " carnivorous amphibia " are the ordinary prey of the sealers, and cannot therefore go into details. All the seals, however, yield a good marketable oil, and the skins are more or less valuable either as furs or for tanning—chiefly the latter. Their flesh, and particularly that of the smaller kinds, although not peculiarly delicate, is fair eating.

Seals are migratory in their habits, but they display an extraordinary attachment to particular spots, to which they will return again and again, although beset with the greatest dangers. They are very tenacious of life, but may readily be stunned by a heavy blow on the nose. Although a seal will always fly from the attack of man if practicable, still, when driven to extremity, it is no despicable foe.

THE DUGONG.

This animal, resembling in form those of the whale tribe, although far smaller, and differing from them in many other respects besides size, is found abundantly on the northern coasts of New South Wales, and is generally known to the colonists as the sea pig.

The head of the dugong is small in proportion to its body, and is most singularly shaped. The upper lip is very thick, and flattened at the extremity. It is to this queer looking snout, we presume, that the animal is indebted for the swinish cognomen by which it is ordinarily known. The dugong has a thick smooth skin, with a few hairs scattered over its surface. Its colour is bluish on the back, with a white breast and belly. In size the full grown male has never, we believe, been found more than eighteen or twenty feet long; but those commonly taken are much less than this.

The food of the dugong consists chiefly of marine vegetables, which it finds at the bottom of inlets, in comparatively shallow water, where it is easily captured. Its flesh resembles good beef, and is much esteemed. The oil obtained from its fat is peculiarly clear and limpid, and is free from any disagreeable smell, such as most animal oils are accompanied with. It has not yet been produced in sufficient quantities to acquire a recognised market value. It was once contemplated, we understand, to bring it into use, with the addition of scent, as a hair oil; and the gentleman who contemplated doing so as a matter of commercial speculation first tried its qualities upon himself. Strange to say, its use was followed by an extraordinary shedding of hair. A trial by the wife of this experimentalist was attended with similar results. It is true that this might have arisen from natural causes, but still the facts point to a different conclusion—a conclusion that, whatever may be our ability to produce a hair oil which shall rival the famous Macassar of Rowland, we can at all events furnish one which shall have the contrary effect of producing baldness.

PART III.

Mines and Mining Operations.

MINERALS AND METALS.

WE have now come to a most important chapter in the history of the natural resources of New South Wales, a chapter abounding in interest, and which must, principally, be devoted, less to the details of the mineral wealth actually in our present possession, than to speculations as to what that wealth may, hereafter, be.

Although scientific men have from a very early period of the history of this colony, predicted its possession of vast mineral treasures, these sources of wealth, have, for the most part, remained undeveloped. The pursuits of agriculture, pasture, and commerce, proved more attractive to the early settlers, and the profits derived from them were so considerable, that they absorbed the whole available labour of the colony.

It may, indeed, be to some matter of surprise that the attractive metalliferous indications which many districts of the colony display, did not induce the British Government, which has always shown the most prompt disposition to take its share of mineral treasures, in whatever part of its dominions they may be found, to attempt the working of mines by means of convict labour, somewhat on the same principle that the Siberian mines are worked for the revenue of the Emperor of Russia. There were, however, many reasons why the Government should not adopt such a course. The immense amount of labour required to open up the colony, even in its earliest limited extent, afforded works of urgent and immediate necessity for all the convicts which it was either prudent or convenient for the Government to retain on its own hand. The assignment system had double recommendations to a government oppressed with the burthen of the cost of its swarms of convicted offenders, and a population rapidly increasing in the amount of its redundancy. Under this system, the English treasury was relieved to a vast extent from the expense attendant on the maintenance of its convicts, after their arrival at the place of their banishment, whilst the labour which was thus at the disposal of the local Government was most valuable as offering a kind of a bounty to the sale of land, and the settlement of the country by a free emigrant class.

Far be it from us to dispute the wisdom of this policy : on the contrary, it would seem a wise dispensation of Providence that the attention of the government was diverted from any minute examination of the enormous mineral wealth which it is now certain exists in the bowels, and even on the surface, of the earth in New South Wales. The civilization and free settlement of these immense and splendid territories, would, in such a case, have been inevitably delayed, if not absolutely prevented. A system of penal slavery would have been made permanent ; a system radically vicious in itself and rendered doubly abominable and oppressive by the insatiable appetite for wealth, which would have increased, year after year, as the stores on which it fed became more abundant. Whether the Government had chosen to work the mines itself, or had farmed them out, after a few years, to private enterprise, convict labour must have been employed, and, once engaged in such a pursuit, the profits derived from such unpaid labour would have been too attractive to be surrendered at any time, without a fierce and destructive struggle. The emancipation of the negroes in the West Indies was, as is well known, resisted with that eagerness which near and touching interest in the matter of dispute alone could engender ; and it could, at last, only be effected by paying a sum, by way of compensation, the liberality of which was, for a time, the wonder of surrounding nations, but which failed to satisfy the planter, or to preserve him from severe distress, and, in many cases, ruin. The same, or a more severe struggle, would have taken place here, where no claim for compensation could have been preferred on account of the cessation of the transportation to these shores of English felons ; but with the urgent desire of the colonists to receive them, there would have been no overtures made by the British Government towards any such cessation, and the evils of the old convict system, exaggerated and increased under the centralization of population, consequent on mining pursuits, would have been indefinitely perpetuated.

Fortunately, then, the discovery of the full importance of our mineral resources was reserved till a later period ; a period when the more attractive, and, it must be added, the more natural, pursuits of labour were fully established in the land ; when the system of transportation, direct to this colony, had altogether ceased for years, and when the last taint that degrading system entailed was rapidly dying out ; and when, instead of tending to increase its evil results, it would serve to put an end to its continuance to any part of these colonies for ever. Established as an enterprising and commercial people, with laws we are ready to acknowledge and obey, with an administration of these laws pure and trusted, because watched by the vigilance of a community anxious to maintain the high character of British institutions, the discovery of vast mineral treasures, it may be hoped, will lead neither to the degrading and slavish indolence which characterizes the Spanish possessions, nor to the reckless licentiousness into

which the lust of gold has betrayed the early
settlers of California. In this colony we ought
to be free from both evils ; all the institutions
which have been tried, and which we believe
are loved and revered in this colony, can be
extended to the gold districts, and unless the
invasion of adventurers be much more numerous and simultaneous than we can possibly
anticipate, we shall be happy and proud to
protect the shelter which these institutions
afford us.

That this colony, that this island continent,
possesses mineral, and particularly metallic,
wealth, in an eminent degree, is now established beyond all doubt ; but to what extent,
and in what variety, is still matter of speculation. Attention was first turned actively to
the surface indications which many districts of
this colony present, by the remarkable effect
which the discovery of the copper mines of
South Australia had in rescuing that colony
from a state of absolute ruin and insolvency
to one of affluence and wealth. South Australia had pasturage for sheep ; she had greater
advantages than this colony possesses for the
growth of grain, but both of these were insufficient to enable her to take an independent
stand among this group of colonies, and in
spite of government patronage, and the most
influential assistance from men of power and
name at home, she must have sunk under her
burden of debt, had it not been for the timely
discovery of the value of her mineral treasures.

It would be beside our purpose here to enter into an account of the success which has attended the working of the South Australian mines; it is sufficient for our purpose to say that that success was sufficient to attract the attention not only of British, but of European capitalists and emigrants, to a falling, to a ruined colony, and to resuscitate that colony from a state of bankruptcy into one of the most flourishing of England's dependencies. Attracted by this success, speculation commenced as to the mineral capabilities of our own colony, and with what success these speculations were attended it will be our duty presently to detail

COAL.

We have stated that it is now established beyond doubt, that Australia abounds with mineral wealth, and we may further state that almost unerring indications of this wealth exist, in every variety, from the commonest, but most useful shape in which it presents itself, namely, that of coal, to the most precious, and the most valuable, that of gold.

We commence, then, with the lower step in the scale of our mineral wealth, the agent, however, by whose assistance alone, we can turn all its more glittering brethren into use and value.

The existence of coal in the immediate vicinity of Sydney was very early discovered, but, in the early years of the colony, for the purpose of clearing the land, wood was used as fuel for almost every purpose. There are but few districts in the colony where coal fields do not, in greater or less degree, prevail, but they exist in the greatest abundance, and exhibit the greatest facility for working, to the north of Sydney, and particularly at the mouth of the Hunter, in the vicinity of Newcastle; in fact, the whole valley of the Hunter is more or less a coal field. The working of the various coal fields in the colony, has, however, been deferred through a variety of circumstances. The use of wood, for fuel, which obtains in all new countries, has prevented a very great demand for coal, and the absence of manufactories, and the mildness of the climate, have prevented the very extensive consumption of fuel, of any description, in proportion to the population of the colony.

But the great obstacle to the development of the coal fields has been the existence of a monopoly in the working of them by the Australian Agricultural Company. Certain coal mines were worked by Government at Newcastle, and, in consideration of certain conditions, these mines were handed over to the company, with a grant of 2000 acres of the coal field at Newcastle, which extends to a great distance, the strata gradually bending down and sinking below the level of the sea. From the period that this grant was made to the Australian Agricultural

Company, the coal in all lands granted or sold by the government was reserved, and the previous grants, in which coal was discovered, were very few. The grant known as Threlkeld's grant, at Lake Macquarie, was worked for some time with considerable success ; and another grant, "Pratt's Grant," was purchased by the Company, who then secured to themselves an entire monopoly in the article. The annual decrease in the amount of firewood in the neighbourhood of Sydney, together with its increased consumption of fuel, from its increased population, the establishment of extensive works and factories, and of steam navigation and gas companies, have increased the consumption of this useful mineral in an extraordinary degree, and the monopoly which was granted in the year 1825, was, about the year 1845, found to be very oppressive. An export trade in coals, had, in the mean time, sprung up, with every prospect of its continuance and increase, and measures were adopted to relieve this branch of the industrial resources of the colony from the restraint to which it was subjected. Various remonstrances against it were agreed to by the legislature of the colony, and, in the year 1847, through the act of the company itself, the sole right of working coal was resigned by the company, and communicated by her Majesty's Secretary of State to the local Government.

From this period the coal trade became free, and the possessors of property on the Hunter, which contained coal easily accessible, began to take measures for turning their hitherto useless wealth to advantage. The discovery of gold in California, about the same time, and the demand which ensued from that country for coal to supply the steamers from Panama and other parts of America, gave a great impetus to the trade, and, in the winter of 1850, the price of coals, in the Sydney market, rose from about 16s. to £2 per ton. Fortunately the freedom which was given to competition soon reduced this exorbitant rate, and the current price of coals, for household purposes, is about 18s. a ton.

In proceeding to examine the nature and extent of the known available coal fields of the colony, and comparing them with our present and probable future consumption, both at home and for exportation, we have procured the information on which we are best able to rely, and have made calculations accordingly.

The coal mines of the Australian Agricultural Company are situated at Newcastle, at the south entrance of an excellent harbour, called Port Hunter. The whole country to the south is an extensive coal field, and presents visible indications, on the most elevated cliffs, of its richness and abundance.

In the year 1836, the total amount of coals produced from these mines was 12,646 tons, which was in fact the whole quantity of coals produced in the colony. As we before stated, the consumption of wood to a large extent in the towns, and exclusively in the country districts, accounts for this apparently very small consumption, as the yield of the mines in later years has tended to show their inexhaustible abundance, and the facility with which the coal may be procured.

In the year 1849, the quantity of coals raised at these mines was 33,390 tons, the estimated official value of which was £10,543 12s. 0d. In 1850, the quantity raised was 45,084 tons, of the estimated official value of £14,615 13s. 0d. In 1851, the quantity raised was 45,642 tons, of the estimated official value of £17,894 4s. 0d.

It will be seen from these returns, that in the year 1849, the estimated value of the coal raised was at the rate of a fraction less than 6s. 6d. per ton, a price which, at the rate at which labour of this description always rules, shows conclusively that the coal fields here are worked with infinitely greater facility, and at infinitely less cost, than those of Great Britain. In 1850, the rate per ton was about 6s. 10½d., the rate of wages being higher, and the demand, both for home consumption and for exportation, having very considerably increased. In 1851, the price had risen to the rate of 7s. 6d. per ton, while, as the quantity raised was not increased, but taken in the aggregate with the produce of other mines, somewhat diminished, it might be imagined that the demand had fallen off. But the fact is, that the demand for coals in the early part of 1851 was so great that the miners made extortionate demands for wages, which were withstood by the proprietors, whilst after the discovery of the gold fields, which took place in April, it was with great difficulty that labour to work the mines was procured at all, and consequently, throughout the year, Sydney and the other towns of the colony were miserably supplied with coal, and that, for the most part, at an exorbitant rate.

In the year 1849, the quantity of coal raised from all other mines save those of the Australian Agricultural Company was 15,126½ tons, at an official value of £4103 12s. 0d., or at the rate of 5s. 6d. per ton. In 1850, the quantity raised was 26,132 tons, of the value of £8760 2s. 0d., being at the rate of 6s. 7d. per ton. In 1851, the quantity raised was 22,018 tons, of the value of £7652 0s. 0d., or at the rate of 7s. per ton. It is somewhat curious to remark, that while the variations in the price, caused by the increase of demand beyond the increase of supply, rule in precisely the same ratio in reference to coals produced from mines generally, as to those produced from the mines of the Company, yet the price obtained by the company has ruled throughout about 7½ per cwt. higher. The prestige of the former monopoly still operates, and it is difficult to imagine what social distress might have been caused by the want of this necessary article for consumption, or what injury our commerce might have sustained, if that most unjust monopoly had been persisted in. The total quantity of coals produced in the years 1849 to 1851, with the official value, was as follows :

	Tons.	£	s.	d.
1849	48,516½	14,647	7	4
1850	71,216½	23,375	15	0
1851	67,660	25,546	8	0

Thus, in the year 1850, the quantity of this most inestimable of the earth's mineral treasures obtained in this colony, was seven times greater than it was in the year 1836, whilst the price, we find, has been reduced since that time from an average of 9s. or 10s. per ton, to an average of from 5s. 6d. to 6s. 6d. per ton.

But large as this increase in production has been, we find that it has not been by any means commensurate with our present demand for consumption. It has been, at various periods for the last two years, almost a matter of favor to obtain coals, even at the extravagant prices asked by the dealers, and it must also be remembered that, even yet, coals are almost unknown as fuel, excepting in the near vicinity of the mines, and in Sydney, where the decrease in the supply of firewood renders them an actual necessary of life. This decrease is going on, and will continue to extend over wide districts, until, on the general clearance of the country round all the towns of the colony, we shall have nothing but coal to resort to as fuel. Even under present circumstances, as we have before said, the increased supply has not met the increased demand, and every year must increase that demand in a twofold degree ; first by the natural increase of consumption by an increasing population, and secondly by the natural decrease of the only substitute which we are likely to find for it in this colony to any extent. Besides these causes of demand, we have also to look to the growing wants of commerce, the growth of manufactures, into which it enters so largely, the supply of steamboats, perhaps of railways, and the incentives to exportation which a high price from foreign nations always affords.

But looking to the most extended development of all these aids to demand, we are not prepared to say that the coal fields at present being worked, would not furnish an almost inexhaustible supply. But, fortunately for this colony, there is no necessity to look to these fields alone. Almost every great district in the colony has been ascertained to possess in abundance this great gift of Providence, and it is in positions, for the most part, of comparatively easy access. To the south, to the west and to the north it is to be found in our ranges in immense quantities, and when enterprise, the desire of gain, or the necessity of their position, shall spur the inhabitants of these districts into action, they will produce it with the like ease, in the like abundance, and with the like profit that the people of the Hunter have done. Newcastle may, like her namesake at home, be the main source of the supply of the metropolis, and her position on the coast enables her to do so with great facility. The coal mines of

Bathurst will not only supply the domestic wants of the district, but by their very richness, combined with the other mineral wealth with which they are closely associated, they will, in course of time, like the Staffordshire mines in England, force into existence towns that will rival the Birminghams, the Wolverhamptons, the Bilstons, and the Dudleys at home.

We have yet a word or two to say in regard to the exportation of coal, and as this has been going on only for a comparatively short time our figures will be necessarily few, but they involve some curious but highly important facts.

The export of coals and coke, in the year 1849, was 10,423 tons, of the value of £4593 ; in 1850, it was 31,461 tons and 2950 bushels, of the value of £15,558 ; in 1851, it was 15,292, tons, of the value of £7550.*

It will be seen from these figures that the export of 1850 was nearly three times as great as it was in 1849, and in 1851 it was only one half as great as in 1850.

The production of coals in each of these latter years was about 70 per cent. greater than in 1849 ; but deduct the export for 1849, the amount left for home consumption was 38,093½ tons. Deducting the exports in 1850, the amount left for home consumption was

---

* The calculations for 1851 are only approximations, the official returns not being made up.

39,755 tons, or, in round numbers, only 1600 tons more than it was in 1849. In 1850, deducting the export, the amount left for home consumption was 52,368 tons.

The coal fields of Australia may then in every sense be looked upon as one of the richest treasures with which she is endowed. Planted beneath and around us in such abundance as to seem like the index hand of Providence, to guide us to manufacturing wealth and commercial greatness—to the dark compact mass which rests beneath the soil do we look in future years for that wealth, which has hitherto flowed so liberally from the scanty vegetation existing upon its surface.

We have examined at some length and in some detail the nature and capacity of our coal mines, because on them must depend in a great measure, the extent to which the metalliferous treasures to which we shall presently refer, can be made available.

MINERALS GENERALLY.

Amongst the more useful and valuable mineral productions of New South Wales, we may mention several kinds of freestone and sandstone, admirably fitted for building purposes. These are found in great abundance all round the coast, and prevail to a great extent in and around the city of Sydney, which might indeed be excavated into one vast quarry. All the public buildings, and in fact almost all stores or houses of any pretension, are built of this stone, which, though in some instances friable from the action of the wind and rain, has for the most part stood well.

There is abundance of clay suited for the making excellent bricks, and in many parts for the manufacture of delf and even porcelain. A considerable quantity of articles of coarse brown delf, such as jars, bottles, &c., are made in the outskirts of the city.

In the interior granite is found extensively through all the ranges, but as yet it has not been much employed for building. Very elegant marbles have been found, some beautifully veined and bearing a high polish. They are used pretty generally in fitting up gentlemen's houses.

Slate has not yet been prepared and used for building purposes, but large beds of it exist in the ranges to the west and north.

A great variety of the lower classes of the precious stones have been found, but hardly yet in sufficient quantities to say whether they may or may not hereafter form an item in the list of the natural treasures of the colony. Reasoning, however, from ordinary analogies, it is probable this will be the case, and that the development of our mines of gold and copper will discover other hidden treasures. Jasper, agate and onyx are frequently met with, and topazes, amethysts, small rubies and emeralds have also been found; but to what extent they exist is at present mere matter of speculation.

R

Among the mineral productions of the country it may, perhaps, be desirable to notice that in the immediate neighbourhood of Sydney, from the geological formation of the district, immense quantities of sand accumulate, of the very finest description for the manufacture of glass. Small quantities of this sand have been sent to England, and have been so highly reported on as to make it somewhat doubtful whether it would not answer to ship it from the colony in large quantities. In addition to this, the abundance of quartz rock throughout the metalliferous districts of the interior, would, if calcined, furnish inexhaustible material for the manufacture of glass of the very best description. In the same way the decomposition of the granite rocks which extend throughout the same districts, produces porcelain clay fit for the manufacture of articles of domestic use, and even for porcelain of the first quality. Here again we find at our hands the material for two most useful and interesting branches of manufacture— manufactures which, while adding to the material wealth of the colony, will encourage art by the rewards they will hold out to colouring and design. In both of these manufactures, too, the abundance of coal on the spot will prove a most advantageous auxiliary.

METALS.

We now proceed to examine the other class of our mineral productions, metals—and in these the colony of New South Wales may be safely declared to vie in wealth with any country in the known world. Wherever metalliferous indications have been displayed, and search has been made, the promise of the surface has been fulfilled, but the search has been made generally in so unscientific and desultory a manner, that the discoveries made have not been turned to profitable account. The want of labour and machinery, the large outlay of capital necessary for procuring both, and the slow returns which must at first be expected from any such investment, compared with those arising from the ordinary pursuits of commerce and agriculture, have deterred enterprise from taking any very energetic or persevering steps in this direction. Still, however, under all these disadvantages, some attempts have been made, which have proved sufficiently the abundance of our metalliferous riches, and have also turned the attention of the colonists here, and commercial men at home, to consider the best means of making those riches available. In the brief limits of these papers it will be impossible to do more than to give a very short and general outline of the metals which have already been discovered, and the nature of the districts in which they are found, but the increased interest which every day affords to geological researches in this colony, will soon furnish the student whose attention may be excited by these pages, with abundant means of information.

IRON.

Iron, the most useful, and the most valuable metal which has been placed in the bowels of the earth for man's use, is ordinarily placed at the bottom of the list, because from the benificient Providence which has supplied it abundantly in most parts of the world, its money value is less in proportion to its weight, than that of any other metal. It is found in great abundance almost throughout the colony of New South Wales, and following the ordinary geological arrangement, is in~~ ~~ ~~throughout~~ with coal. In the coal fields ~~the~~ River, iron ore of good quality prevails very largely, but it has not hitherto, been worked. In the western district, round Bathurst, which may, in fact, be pre-eminently distinguished as the metalliferous district of the colony, it is found very abundantly, and the ores are of the very highest character, such as magnetic oxides, bog iron, &c. Along the Southern Road too, iron ore of a similar valuable description has been found plentifully, and one mine, called the Fitz Roy Mine, has been opened, and on a small scale successfully worked. It is situated in the dividing range of mountains in the vicinity of the hill well known to travellers on the Southern Road as the Razorback. The iron produced from this mine has proved to be of the highest quality, and from it very superior articles of cutlery have been manufactured in the colony. But to make the speculation a good one, a very large outlay would be necessary, particularly as at present there are no coal fields worked in the vicinity. Blast furnaces would have to be erected, with all the apparatus of rollers and tilts for manufacturing the iron into bars, sheets, or hoops, and as these would have to be imported, a preliminary expenditure of capital of from £20,000 to £30,000 would be absolutely necessary, and we see but little chance of any such expenditure being made at present. In fact, any such investment would not and the slo.... for many years. The roads of expect.... must first be improved to facilitate carriage; and the formation of railroads both in the laying down the roads themselves, and in the machinery employed upon them, will increase the demand for iron till it grows to that extent that our own exigencies will force upon us the necessity of appealing to our own productive resources. At present, and probably for many years to come, the process of smelting is carried on by using green timber and charcoal for fuel, and the ore run in this manner naturally possesses nearly all the qualities of steel. We have seen very excellent pocket knives, and even surgical instruments, made from iron manufactured in this manner, and which is subjected to no subsequent process of refining.

In some of the remoter districts, iron for the use of the stations, in the formation of farming implements, &c., has, in some rare instances, at the suggestion of scientific men, been manufactured in the same way as it is in the interior of the Brazils, and, I believe, in South Africa. As the process is not, perhaps, very generally known, and it may be advantageously disseminated throughout the colony, it may not be out of place to describe it here.

In a common smith's forge a space is cleared out about four inches below the hole through which the blast of the bellows enters the fireplace. About eighteen inches from this hole a clay form is made to keep the fire together, and a strong fire of charcoal is blown up. A quantity of from 70 lbs. to 100 lbs. of fine iron ore, crushed to powder, is then strewed into the fire, for the first hour and a half at the rate of about four lbs. every ten minutes, and during the next two hours the remainder is gradually strewn in. A strong fire must be kept up for two hours and a half longer, making six hours altogether. Some ores will require more, and some less time in this smelting process, and some will require lime to be strewed into the fire. In the Brazils five or six forges are frequently thus kept at work by a fall of water. When the iron is sufficiently heated (in its glowing liquid state) the top layer of charcoal is taken off, and when the mass cools, the lump of pure malleable iron remains with fragments of charcoal adhering to it, which are then broken off. It may then be hammered out on the anvil to any size that may be required. This process also is sometimes effected by large hammers worked by a water-wheel, but more frequently by hand with sledge hammers. Of iron smelted this way horse-shoe nails may be made so pliable that they may be bent between the fingers. And borers and other tools may be made, which by plunging them in cold water when hot (not quite at a red heat) will answer all the purposes of common work without steeling. In fact, by care in tempering the iron during the process of working, any degree of hardness may be attained. A French gentleman of the name of A. St. Miguel, in the province of Menas Geries, supplies the mines with stamp heads of wrought iron, of the weight of 300 lbs. each, which will last as long as three English cast iron ones.

There can be little doubt that this system of smelting for individual use might be advantageously carried out. In most districts iron-stone is found on the very surface of the earth, and though it might require some little patience to make experiments in order to ascertain the nature of the ore, this would soon be achieved, and the process then would be perfectly simple. With the abundant leisure which appertains to most persons in the bush, this plan suggests a useful and economical occupation of time, and we confess we should like to see it extend in the colony, as it would give an impulse to the manufacture and use of metals. We believe that this system, simple as it may seem, was the original foundation of iron smelting in England, and to these clay furnaces may be traced those huge establishments, the roar of whose blasts and the glare of whose fires rival the terrors and the wonders of the craters of volcanoes.

We have in the course of this digression alluded to the use of lime as necessary in the process of smelting some descriptions of iron ores. Lime is an essential ingredient in the smelting of most metallic ores, and is, therefore, fortunately dispersed in large quantities over most of the metalliferous regions of this country.

LEAD.

At present we have no lead mine in process of working, nor indeed has search been made for this metal to sufficient extent to enable us to state positively that any lead mine (properly so called) exists; but there is very little doubt about the matter. In the Bathurst district indications of lead in considerable quantities occur, but it is principally in connection with other metals, and geologists seem generally to incline to the opinion, that for the production of lead alone, it will not pay to work the veins which have been discovered.

TIN.

There have been frequent rumours of the discovery of tin mines in various parts of the colony, and similar reports have also arisen

with regard to South Australia ; but we do not
think that in any part of this island continent
either the selfish (we use the word in no sense
of disparagement) researches of the adventurer,
or the discoveries of the scientific geologist, as
yet justify the opinion that tin mines of any
richness or productiveness will be found.   In
a country, however, so rich in mineral treasures, and so remarkable for the unmistakeable
nature of its surface indications of those treasures, it would be presumptuous to say that
this valuable and useful metal may not very
shortly be added to our list of products.

COPPER.

Perhaps the most striking metalliferous
feature of the Australasian continent is the
abundant indications which display themselves in almost every direction of the existence of copper. In almost all the ranges
these indications prevail in a greater or less
degree, sometimes in one variety of ore and
sometimes in another, and not unfrequently in
nearly a pure state, as if the native metal had
been smelted by the operation of subterranean
heat.

In the southern part of the continent these
indications are the most rich, and as yet they
have in that district proved themselves the
true index of metallic wealth.   In the province
of South Australia, there were in the year
1851   upwards of sixty mining companies

established, more than fifty of which invested their capital in copper mining. Some of these mines have proved very rich, and the original proprietors have amassed immense sums of money, either by working the mines themselves or disposing of them to English and Colonial Joint-stock Companies. The Burra Burra Mines are perhaps the richest copper mines in the known world, at least as far as the yield has at present developed itself. Besides the very large shipments of ore which have been made to Europe, there were no less than five large smelting establishments in active operation in the province. We use the past tense in speaking of these Mining and Smelting Companies, because from the enormous emigration which has taken place from the province to the sister colonies in consequence of the gold discoveries, many of the works are for the present abandoned. There is no labour to work the mines, and the wealth which has sustained the province for the last ten years, and which has enabled her to progress in population and importance, with almost unequalled rapidity, now lies dormant on the earth. To the same cause may be attributed the comparatively little success which has attended mining operations in this colony.

The prevalence of other pursuits, and the deficiency of labour which prevailed, even for the successful prosecution of them, left none for the laborious enterprise of mining.

In South Australia copper became the staple article of export, and upon it depended the prosperity of the country. In New South Wales, wool, tallow, and other pastoral and agricultural produce, were the means of wealth.

Consequently, mining operations were few, and of very limited extent. Still, however, several private proprietors, and one or two companies, have opened mines, and have worked them with considerable success.

The principal copper district yet known in the colony is in the Western District, around Bathurst; at Carcoar, Molong, the Cornish Settlement, Wellington, and Yass. The principal mines yet opened are, the Coombing Mine, about two miles south-west of Carcoar, the Cornish Settlement Copper Mines, the Molong Mines, and the Belubula Mines.

In all these mines shafts have been sunk, and a considerable quantity of ore raised. These ores are of a valuable kind, and of great variety, and indicate the existence of copper in vast quantities. More conspicuously among them are found silicate of copper, blue and green carbonate, phosphate, red oxide of copper, black oxide of copper, manganese, pyrites, and tile copper ore. At several of these mines smelting works have been erected, and the process of smelting with green timber is carried on successfully.

This last operation is of very great importance, for rich as the ores raised are on all hands admitted to be, the distance from the sea coast, and the state of the roads in the colony at present, would prevent them being brought to a port of shipment with any profit. The want of skilled labour to work the mines has been severely felt, and mistakes have been made from want of knowledge and experience, which have tended to cast discredit on the mines, and to bring their richness in question. During the last two years, however, a good number of miners have been imported from England, and when the gold fever has, in some measure, subsided, there can be little doubt that unpretending copper will form as valuable an item in the products of the colony.

GOLD.

We now come to the first of metals, and in the present state of excitement it is almost difficult to state calmly and concisely the facts connected with the first discovery, and the present search for this metal.

Scientific men, both in the colony and in Europe, have predicted for some years past, from the geological indications of the country, that many of the mountainous ranges of the Australian Continent would be found to be auriferous.

They were similar in character to the mountains of the other gold districts, both in Europe and in America.

In speaking on this subject the Reverend W. B. Clarke, a geologist of high scientific attainments, and who for many years past has been deeply engaged in the study of the geology of this colony, makes the following observations : — " Years ago gold was found in small specimens by the earlier convicts ; but the value of the indications was not then known, and the facts were concealed. In 1841, the author of these remarks again brought gold from the very basin of the river now supplying it (the Macquarie). This gold was exhibited to the members of the Government and of the Legislature in the Council Chamber itself. and to numbers of persons in the community who have testified to the fact : it was spoken of openly ; it has been discussed in public journals ; it was made the ground of enquiries into the probable extensive auriferous character of the colony, and from the result of those enquiries, conducted on scientific principles, and backed by occasional additional proofs, it was openly declared that gold exists " in *considerable abundance* in our schists and quartzites" ; and further, the very region was pointed out in which it would be found. Still no one seemed willing to profit by the disclosure, made as it was cautiously for reasons which can be appreciated when it is considered that the country was still a penal settlement. The fact was not doubted, but the public mind was directed to another channel. So in England, though an illustrious geologist (Sir R. Murchison) had declared his suspicion that Australia offered in some respects a parallel to the Ural, and though another in Russia had done the same, and though the former had spoken so late as 1849 to the Ministers of England upon the subject of gold in Australia, all the encouragement he received was in being told not to let them *" have too much of a good thing."*

It will be seen then, notwithstanding the overwhelming surprise with which the late discovery has been regarded, both by the colonists themselves, and by Europeans, that amongst men acquainted with the geological formation of the country, men of science, and even by men moving in official circles, the announcement of " the great fact" must have been in some measure, looked for. But there were many and cogent reasons, why the knowledge possessed on the subject should be allowed to remain unfruitful. We believe, even among scientific men, while they were satisfied of the auriferous character of the rocks of the Australian cordillera, there existed very considerable doubt as to the precious metal being found in any such quantities as would lead to gold seeking ever becoming a profitable pursuit. The British Colonial Government, ever averse to any changes which might disturb official laziness, cared not to encourage the discovery of so fruitful a bone of contention as the precious metals in this distant, enterprising, and enthusiastic community ; the offered wealth was encumbered with all the accompaniments of royalties, territorial regulations, and prerogative rights, and all the mass of grumbling disaffection and resistance which have ever followed in their train. They, therefore, were content to leave New South Wales to grow fat on its wool and tallow, believing, and probably with much truth, that in so doing they would be better providing a favourable field for the redundant population of the mother country. Amongst the colonial community, too, there were many causes why these foretellings should have been regarded coldly. Those who had large stakes in the colony, whose capital was invested in agricultural or pastoral pursuits, would naturally look not only with distrust, but with dismay, at the introduction of a pursuit the attractions of which would necessarily absorb that scant labour on which their very existence was dependent. Among the rich then, the selfish law of self-preservation was at work, while among the poor, in their minds, the idea of men picking up gold in gullies and on the banks of rivers, of washing earth in tin dishes or rocking it in cradles, had not yet found a local habitation. To tell them that because the primary rocks were displaced from their usual order in this colony—that quartz and schist were found on the surface—that therefore gold was to be had for the seeking, was to make them smile in wonder and contempt.

The wonderful discovery in California soon

however put an end to this ignorance. The mystery, as to the pursuit of gold digging, was dispelled, and thousands on thousands hurried across mighty deserts and rolling oceans, to gather every man for himself his share of the golden treasure. This colony felt the impetus, and without pausing to consider the prognostications of the existence of similar riches here, hundreds and thousands rushed to the American Dorado, leaving behind them the treasure caves of the Australian mountains, doomed still for a little period to remain closed and sealed. But the public mind was now alive to the subject of gold finding, and in 1850, a word, a hint, a suspicion of the existence of gold, was stronger than the most complete and satisfactory deductions of science in 1840.

An adventurer from New South Wales to California was struck by the similarity of the formation of the gold districts of California to those which he had traversed in the county of Bathurst in this colony. He wrote to a friend in Sydney, assuring him he could point out a gold field in New South Wales. The conviction grew upon him stronger and stronger, till at last, quitting the successful pursuit of gold in California, impelled by an irresistible faith in the opinion he had formed, he arrived in the colony. Almost without means he commenced what all his friends thought his visionary search, and after many disappointments and severe trials, in the month of

May, 1851, Edward Hammond Hargraves announced and unmistakeably proved, that New South Wales was to take its place amongst the richest gold countries of the known globe.

Mr. Hargraves did not pretend to arrive at his conclusion, that gold was to be found in New South Wales, on any very precise scientific deductions. It was the surface indications in the first place that struck him, and the similarity of these indications in California and in Australia was so great, that he could not resist the opinion that if gold was to be found in one, it was in the other also. Mr. Hargraves, however, had the opportunity of digging and seeing others dig successfully for gold in California, and thus when he came here to try the same experiment, and found the same formations in the same position, he was the more encouraged in his undertaking. He was geologist sufficient to distinguish these formations one from another, and rightly judged that if the quartz veins of the mountain ranges in California produced gold, they would be likely to do so elsewhere.

To the scientific geologist, however, the analogy displayed in the Australian cordillera to other prolific gold producing countries was so striking, that it could hardly fail to ensure conviction. The same rocks which produced gold in other countries, were found in Australia under the same normal conditions. The mountain ranges in the gold district, (the

western counties) exhibit the same disturbances
in their geological formation as exist in the
Ural mountains and in California; while the
same minerals, metals, and fossils are found in
abundance in all.

The same evidence which leads us to the
conclusion that gold exists in Australia, would
also tend to the belief that it is distributed in
considerable quantities, not here and there in
isolated spots, but throughout the ranges
where the same derangement of the primary
rocks prevails, and this conclusion has been
the more firmly established by the discovery
of gold in great abundance, under similar indications, in the province of Victoria. The
field, in fact, seems almost illimitable, and
calculation grows into speculation in
any effort to determine the results which may
ensue from it.

The discovery of Mr. Hargraves was announced to the colonists on the 8th May, 1851.
The field he had discovered was in the county
of Wellington, at the foot of what is called the
"Big Hill." These diggings, extending over a
very considerable district, have subsequently
been termed the Ophir diggings, and although
their early richness has somewhat declined,
there is little reason to doubt that they will
yet prove of enormous wealth, under the development which skill and capital will afford.
The gold is found principally in the bed and on
the banks of creeks—generally tributaries of
the river Macquarie.

Early in June, gold was reported by the Colonial Geologist (Mr. Stutchbury) to exist in considerable abundance at the junction of the Turon and Macquarie rivers, and this having been discovered to be true, a very large number of gold seekers repaired there, and the banks of the Turon and the numerous creeks which are tributary to it, have since been the principal point of attraction to the diggers of New South Wales. In June, 1851, 600 licenses were granted by the government to dig in these localities, and in July 1500. In a month or two after, as many as 5000 or 6000 people were assembled at the Turon, and for some time the yield must have averaged very considerably over 10,000 ounces a week. A township was established called Sofala, and it is now a thriving and considerable place.

The search for gold now, however, prevailed in every district in the colony, and not a day passed without the news of some fresh discovery appearing in the colonial journals. Many of these reports were, doubtless, much exaggerated, and probably in some instances entirely unfounded ; but it is very likely that in most instances small quantities of gold were found, and though the search for more, may have as yet been un uccessful, because unskilfully prosecuted, these scattered localities may yet prove to be very rich in the precious metal.

The discovery of gold at the Meroo Creek,

in the beginning of July, 1851, which falls into the Cudgegong River about fifteen miles above its junction with the Macquarie, was the next step of material importance in the gold dis covery. The discovery was in this spot made by an aboriginal native, who having informed his master (Dr. Kerr) of the circumstance, the latter proceeded to the spot, and at once secured several large blocks of quartz richly impregnated with gold. The largest of these blocks weighed 76 lbs. and yielded 60 lbs. of pure gold. The whole quantity of gold and quartz together weighed about 300 lbs., and the quantity of pure gold extracted from it was 106 lbs., the largest quantity of gold, we believe, ever discovered in one mass. The gold dis-covered by Dr. Kerr, with the exception of some specimens kept by him, was sold for £4160.

From this period a considerable number of diggers have attended at Meroo Creek and a considerable quantity of gold has been extracted, but it is expected that very rich results may be looked for from the investment of capital in gold operations in this locality.

The spot on which the large mass we have alluded to was found has been leased to an association of persons who intend establishing a quartz-crushing establishment there.

About the same period gold was discovered in considerable abundance at Louisa Creek, another tributary of the Macquarie, and a con-siderable number of men have since been em-ployed there.

In October, 1851, diligent search having been made for months previously, an extensive gold field was discovered in the southern district of the country, in the county of St. Vincent, and this is now a favorite resort of the diggers, who are at present employed on two creeks running into the river Araluen. The yield from these diggings is very extensive, and an escort for the conveyance of the gold to Sydney has been established.

But by far the richest gold field yet discovered in Australia, is to be found still further to the south, in the province of Victoria. Gold was first discovered in any quantity in this province, at Mount Ballarat, in the county of Grant, where the yield was found to be very great, and the gold of fine quality. These diggings, however, were soon, in a great measure, superseded by the discovery of a field of unexampled wealth at Mount Alexander, to the north-west of Melbourne. The immense quantity of gold found here, attracted thousands of adventurers from the neighbouring colonies, and it is computed at the present time there are not less than 50,000 persons employed at these diggings.

The quality of the gold discovered at all the Australian fields is considered very fine, very much of it being considerably over standard gold. The price it has fetched in the colony generally may be said to have averaged about £3 6s.— but this price has been less governed by the positive value of the gold than by the pressure on the money market occasioned by the accession of so enormous an amount to the exportable produce of the colony.

The value of the gold shipped from Sydney up to the present time, 1st April 1852, is £1,200,000, but a large allowance is to be made in this for gold received from Victoria. Up to the 1st April 1852 the amount of gold produced in the province of Victoria was 563,471 ounces – the value of which in the colony, say at the rate of £3 5s. per oz., is £1,831,081. There is however little reason to doubt that new and abundant fields will be in continual course of discovery, in fact several districts have been pointed out by the scientific gentlemen employed by the government, which have all the indications of being highly auriferous.

The regulations under which gold is allowed to be dug for may be briefly described as follows:

All persons digging or searching for alluvial gold, to take out a license, the license fee being at the rate of £1 10s. 0d. per month. All gold procured without due authority is liable to seizure, in whose possession soever it be. Persons applying for license, require to prove they are not absent from hired service. Claims to work unoccupied ground to be marked out on the following scale:

1. Fifteen feet frontage to either side of a river or main creek.

2. Twenty feet of the bed of a tributary to

a river or main creek, extending across its whole breadth.

3. Sixty feet of the bed of a ravine or water course.

4. Twenty feet square of table land or river flats.

These claims to be secured to parties only as they may continue to hold licenses for the same, except in case of flood or accident. Licenses liable to be cancelled on conviction of the holders of selling spirits, or of any disorderly and riotous conduct. Persons found working alluvial gold, on public or private lands, without a license, to pay a double license fee. Disputes as to claims to be settled by the Commissioners. Licenses to dig on lands alienated from the crown, to be issued only to the proprietors, or persons authorized by the proprietors in writing to apply for the same. The fee for such licenses to be 15s. per month. Licenses for draining ponds and water holes, for the purpose of obtaining alluvial gold, to be obtainable on paying as many license fees as shall be proportioned to the area of the water hole—calculating twenty-five feet square for every license. Reservoirs and dams for the purpose of washing gold, to be constructed on the permission of the Commissioners. Owners of claims employing labourers and paying license fees for them, allowed to transfer such licenses to other labourers. All persons searching for matrix gold, by working auriferous quartz veins, to pay a royalty of ten per cent. on all gold obtained, to an officer appointed by the Government. The party working the vein to come under a bond in the sum of £1000 to pay such royalty, the Government officer to reside on the land, and to have access to the buildings and premises and to all books and accounts connected with the production of gold. All buildings, and machinery, erected on the land to be considered as additional security to the Government. The claim to consist of half a mile, and in the course of the vein, with a quarter of a mile on each side of the vein reserved for building purposes, &c. The right to cut timber and to use water on the land to be granted; the claim to be forfeited by neglecting to pay the prescribed royalty; by not employing twenty persons or machinery, calculating one horse power to seven men, within six months after the application for the claim has been accepted; or by ceasing to employ that number subsequently; by the employment of unlicensed persons to work alluvial gold on the claim, or violating in any way the terms of the bond. The duration of the claims to be three years, to be extended further under instructions from Her Majesty's government, if the conditions of the bond have all been fulfilled. No portion of land, previously occupied and claimed for alluvial gold, will be open for selection for matrix gold while it continues to be worked for the former. The royalty for working auriferous quartz on private lands to be five per cent. Persons occupying portions of the gold field for trading purposes, to pay a license fee of £1 10s. 0d. per month.

The life of the gold digger is very hard and laborious, and is subject to many hardships and privations. At the Turon and Ophir diggings the operations are often suspended by overwhelming floods, while down at Mount Alexander, the most distressing state of things prevails from the want of water for the ordinary purposes of life.

The equipment of the gold digger is simple, even to rudeness clad in his red or blue wollen shirt, fustian trowsers, and hat of any material or shape, varying to suit either the fancy or the convenience of the wearer; his outer man presents a wild and somewhat savage appearance. A light tent made of oiled calico is his shelter, and wrapped in his blanket, he here sleeps with that soundness which hard labour and fatigue are sure to produce. The shovel pointed at the end—the pick short and stout, crow-bars of different sizes, tin dishes, buckets to carry earth and water in, and the cradle, form the apparatus of the alluvial gold digger. Of course when capital shall be extensively employed, the machinery will be much more complicated and expensive, but we believe the returns will be proportionately large and much more certain.

It is a gratifying fact, and one with which we are happy to be able to conclude this paper, that contrary to the experience of all

v

ages, in other auriferous countries, the discovery of gold in New South Wales has not induced any lawlessness or disorder ; nor has it superseded the ordinary pursuits of the country. On the contrary, there is every reason to hope that by the stimulus which will be given to population and capital in the colony by this discovery, increased energy will be given to those branches of industry which have hitherto so successfully advanced our position amongst British dependencies.

PART IV.

Agriculture—Horticulture—the Vine, and its products.

AGRICULTURE.

THE pursuit of agriculture has never been a favorite one in this colony. This has arisen not as some would have it from any scarcity of arable land, but from the greater profit and consequently greater attraction to capitalists of other avocations—pastoral and commercial. The occasional droughts, too, and the heavy losses which they sometimes entail upon the agriculturist, deter many from entering upon this branch of industry.

There are few of the class designed emphatically "the farmers" in England. The agriculturists of Australia are for the most part either gentlemen who carry on a little farming as an adjunct to other pursuits, or persons cultivating small portions of land either their own property or held at low rents from some of the great proprietors. A great deal of land is held upon what are termed clearing leases — the removal of the timber and the subjection of the land being held equivalent to rent, and a nominal payment only being exacted for the purpose of asserting the proprietorship. The simplicity of this species of tenancy and the little outlay which is required on the part of the tenant renders it advantageous to a certain extent; but it has its evils. The tenant invests no capital in his undertaking; generally speaking he has little or none to invest. A few implements of husbandry, and a little store of salt beef, flour, tea, and sugar are sufficient to start him in his enterprise, and for a habitation, a hut of bark, or at best of slabs, erected with his own hands, is deemed sufficient. Just so much labour and skill as are necessary to procure remunerative crops with as little delay as possible are applied, but no more. But little attention is paid to scientific principles, even if the farmer knows anything about them, which is not often the case, and consequently the lands of better quality are often completely exhausted. In short it is the interest of the tenant to make the most of his holding, and with the least possible trouble, during the time it is in his possession, without reference to its permanent improvement.

The extreme simplicity of farming operations in New South Wales is, indeed, one of their chief characteristics. Chemical science and mechanical aids, as applied to these operations by the cultivators of Europe, are but little understood and still less resorted to. In the case of drought, for instance, much evil might be warded off with a little care and industry. There are many situations where a complete system of irrigation might be carried out with a very small outlay, and yet the farmers prefer to go on as heretofore—trusting to Providence and grumbling throughout the dry seasons. There are very many exceptions, no doubt, and in some cases the force of example has brought about a better system of cultivation throughout whole neighbourhoods; but taken as a class, the farmers of New South Wales adhere to the more primitive methods, and trouble themselves very little about either chemistry or mechanics.

Agriculture has not, like many other pursuits, progressed in a rate corresponding to the increase of the population, but nevertheless, it *has* progressed to a very material extent. Formerly we were dependent almost wholly upon foreign supplies for our bread stuffs. At present, although not wholly independent of these supplies, our position in this respect has very greatly improved. The published official returns extend only to the 31st December, 1850, and include the colony of Victoria, then known by the more humble appellation of the Port Philip District. They form, however, a very fair guide, for although the population of the two colonies has been materially increased since the gold discoveries, the pickaxe and cradle have proved so much more attractive than the plough and harrow, that there has, upon the whole, been little if any extension of agricultural operations. But it is doubtful whether there has been much diminution, especially in New South Wales proper; for the bulk of those who had farmsteads, contrived, even in the midst of their gold-hunting speculations, to look sharply after seed time and harvest, rightly judging that the coveted metal was more likely to be procured by these means than by any other. If some of the farming class neglected their legitimate pursuits altogether, others on the contrary extended them, which would keep matters pretty even.

In 1843 there were imported 395,374 bushels of wheat, 583 bushels of maize, 61,361 bushels of barley, oats, and peas, 6,941,760 lbs. of flour and bread, 547 tons of potatoes, and 1,678,208 lbs. of rice; the value of the whole, as entered in the returns of imports, being £112,387. In the course of the same year there were exported 273 bushels of wheat, 4687 bushels of maize, 1870 bushels of barley, oats and peas, 3,146,192 lbs. of flour and bread, and 47 tons of potatoes. Official value of the whole £13,486. Thus the excess in value of imports over exports during that year was £98,901.

In 1850, there were imported 84,562 bushels of wheat, 100 bushels of maize, 71,896 bushels of barley, oats, and peas, 2,551,842 lbs. of flour and bread, 917,952 lbs. of rice, and 1524 tons of potatoes. Official value of the whole £32,162. During the same year, there were exported 6964 bushels of wheat, 1712 bushels of maize, 20,526 bushels of barley, oats, and peas, 5,003,078 lbs. of flour and bread, and 52 tons potatoes. Official value of the whole £24,204. In this year, therefore, the excess of imports over exports was only £7958.

The quantity of land under cultivation in 1843, exclusive of gardens and orchards, was as follows: Under wheat, 78,083 acres, yielding 1,000,225 bushels; under maize, 29,061 acres, yielding 719,358 bushels; under barley, 5727 acres, yielding 95,658 bushels; under rye, 514 acres, yielding 5145 bushels; under oats, 4537 acres, yielding 92.268 bushels; under millet, 42 acres, yielding 410 bushels; under potatoes, 5872 acres, yielding 16,392 tons; under tobacco, 655 acres, yielding 6098 cwt; under sown grasses oats, and barley for hay, 21,162 acres, yielding 27,774 tons.   The total number of acres under crop during this year, was 145,653; and the population at this time, numbered 165,541 souls.

The same returns for the year 1850, show the following results.   Quantity of land under crop for wheat, 99,230 acres, yielding a produce of 1,477,749 bushels; under maize, 23,197 acres, yielding 457,106 bushels; under barley, 9740 acres, yielding 164,768 bushels; under oats, 7790 acres, yielding 152,848 bushels; under rye, 293 acres, yielding 5529 bushels; under millet, 42 acres, yielding 848 bushels; under potatoes, 7074 acres, yielding 15,012 tons; under tobacco, 510 acres, yielding 4923 cwt.; under sown grasses, oats, and barley for hay, 49,948 acres, yielding 65,731 tons.   The total number of acres under crop during the year, was 196,824, and the population at this time numbered 265,503 souls.

These returns, as already stated, do not include either gardens or orchards, neither do they include the vineyards which are now scattered over the whole face of the country, and from which one of its most valuable products is obtained.

There is, besides, a good deal of cultivation in the pastoral districts of the interior of which no returns are furnished. Few stations of any magnitude are without their "cultivation paddocks," where grain and vegetables are raised for the use of the squatter and his establishment, and sometimes tobacco for sheep-dressings. Agricultural operations are greatly restricted in the pastoral districts by the working of the Government regulations, which, not only prohibit the *sale*, but even the *exchange* of the produce thus raised upon lands held under depasturing licenses. Agriculture, therefore, may be described as an operation from hand to mouth, as far as these districts are concerned. Still at very many stations the amount of cultivation is quite respectable. Large, well-managed, and tastefully laid out gardens are common, and even tolerable orchards and vineyards—of course on a small scale—are occasionally met with.

Around the metropolis, as well as in the vicinity of most of the larger towns, are many highly-improved market gardens and orchards, to say nothing of those attached to the mansions of the rich, and the cottages of the poor; and cultivated as a matter of scientific and tasteful recreation, or as a relief from more severe and oppressive toil.

The extent of the colony, and the variations of temperature in different parts of it, owing as well to a variance in altitude, as to a variance in geographical position, have given it peculiar advantages for agricultural and horticultural purposes. There is, probably, no known production of the vegetable world which might not be raised in some parts of New South Wales. Even as it is, there are few fruits and vegetables which may not, when in season, be procured at a cheap rate in the Sydney markets, and those which are at present most scarce, are grown in abundance, and without difficulty, at no great distance. gooseberries, for instance, which can be raised only by very great care near Sydney, owing to the warmth of the climate, are excellent and abundant about Goulburn, and even nearer. The contemplated railway between Sydney and Goulburn will be the means, among other and greater advantages, therefore, of bringing us an abundant supply of this fruit. At present it is found cheaper to import gooseberries from Van Diemen's Land.

Many experiments have been made of late, with a view to the development of new agricultural resources. Some have proved failures, but more have turned out satisfactorily. Others again, either from having been only partially tried or badly managed, have not led to results sufficiently definite to warrant any distinct assertion as to whether they have failed or succeeded. Cotton, for instance, has been raised with such facility, and of such excellent quality, that there is scarcely a doubt of its becoming ultimately a valuable and important export. The sugar cane, too, has been cultivated with success in the northern districts, but whether it will be possible to produce sugars sufficiently cheap to compete with those of Manila, or with the sugar producing communities of Polynesia, which are just beginning to struggle for a footing in the markets of the southern hemisphere, is very doubtful.

Practical agriculture in New South Wales differs in many essentials from practical agriculture in Great Britain. The "farming man" from the latter country, therefore, has a good deal to learn, and some little, perhaps, to unlearn before he can be said to have completed his training for agricultural pursuits at the antipodes. The variations in climate—the reversal of the seasons—the peculiar features and qualities of the untilled lands—and the difficulty of procuring many of the necessary dressings, are the principal causes of the difference alluded to.

Of course there are very many persons who, having thoroughly mastered all these local difficulties, are in a position to impart to others the necessary instruction. And there is no unwillingness to do this. But the tyro cannot go rambling about the country from homestead to homestead, in search of information ; and there are unfortunately no works of instruction upon this subject to be procured. Many exceedingly valuable papers on the subject of agriculture appear from time to time in the public journals ; but, as everybody knows, these journals are themselves ephemeral, and the lessons of practical wisdom and experience imparted through their columns, necessarily partake of the same character. Consequently they pass into oblivion without leaving behind them a record of their existence. A series of very able papers on the subject of grain culture, from the pen of a gentleman occupying perhaps the highest place among the promoters and guardians of agriculture in the colony, appeared a year or two ago in the *Herald*. An excellent little pamphlet upon cotton growing—clear, practical, and unassuming—has been issued by Mr. Gardiner, of the Hunter River district, and there have been several other productions of a similar character ; to say nothing of the various letters from correspondents in the newspapers, and the reports and addresses, &c., at meetings of the different associations from time to time for the encouragement of agriculture, horticulture, vine growing, and other pursuits of a similar nature. That which is wanted, and greatly wanted too, is a complete practical work, containing a synopsis of all these scattered materials.

It is to be hoped that some such work will be undertaken ere long. It would, however, be beyond the scope of these papers to do more than touch lightly upon the leading characteristics of the various branches of production and productive industry to which they refer.

Two things have ever been impressed, by the best authorities, upon persons entering into farming operations in New South Wales : first not to enter upon this pursuit until they have sufficient capital, not only to procure a decent outfit in the way of agricultural implements, &c., but to maintain themselves for about a year and a half independently of their crops : secondly, to eschew the slovenly mode of culture, such as sowing grain with the tree stumps in the ground, &c., which is too often practised in the colony, and to clear and fence every acre of land before cropping it.

Farms do not very often change hands in this part of the world, so that the new beginner has generally to commence his operations upon the virgin soil. Open forest land is that which is generally selected for agricultural purposes. This has consequently to be cleared. There are two ways of clearing land: first, by grubbing up trees at their roots, reducing them into logs with a cross-cut saw, and burning these logs in heaps : secondly, by "ringing" or "girdling" the trees, that is, destroying them by a circular incision through the bark, and burning them as they stand. The latter, being the least expensive process, is the one most commonly resorted to, except in cases where a speedy clearing, without reference to expense, is the primary object. The "ring" is cut through the the outer and inner barks; a strip of about half a foot wide being cut entirely away. If this is carefully and efficiently done when the sap is up, the tree soon dies, and a deep hole being cut away at the roots, it is left standing until it has become sufficiently dry for burning. This is about a year or a year and a half after the ringing. Fire is applied at the roots in the holes dug for this purpose, and speedily does its work if the trees be dry enough. When the operation of burning has been completed, the ashes and burnt soil are spread over the land, and increase very materially its productive capacity.

The papers upon grain culture, already mentioned, contain many earnest protestations against the slovenly modes of culture, which have grown up in this colony, and point out with much force, the advantages derivable from strict adherence to a better system. One of the points thus urged, is, that land should be harrowed immediately after ploughing, instead of being left exposed to the influences of the sun and wind, which, in such a climate as this, must harden the clods and render the work of harrowing more difficult, besides depriving the soil of a good deal of its moisture, and perhaps of some of its principles of fertility. In this and many other respects, particularly in the details of maize culture, there seems to be an almost incredible amount of carelessness and inattention among the colonial farmers.

The climate of Australia, notwithstanding its dryness, affords very great advantages to the husbandman ; for he may have here two principal grain crops at exactly opposite periods of the year ; he may sow wheat in April and May, and maize in October and November, and in the interim between these two periods, he may sow barley, rye, and various kinds of pulse.

The growth of maize and wheat alternately, has been found more advantageous and profitable than the growth of wheat alone ; and maize has the advantage of being grown with comparatively little trouble, and without any demand for skilled labour. It is very profitable also, bearing heavy crops, particularly if the soil be rich. Over a hundred bushels of grain to the acre have been raised upon highly manured land, and sixty bushels to the acre is an ordinary product of the more prolific kinds of Indian corn.

But the great fault with the Australian farmers, and particularly with those commonly called the "small farmers," is that they are content to plod on in a settled routine, ploughing and harrowing, sowing and reaping, as their fathers have done before them, and as their neighbours are doing around them, without availing themselves of the aids which the progress of science in latter years has placed within their power ; or turning their attention to other sources of production, not only within their reach, but within what may be termed the boundaries of their occupation. It is hard to coax them out of their beaten paths. In some parts of the country a good deal of tobacco has indeed been grown, and with profit, but it is asserted by those who are presumed to be best acquainted with this branch of agricultural industry, that there is considerable room for improvement in the system usually pursued by the growers. The culture of the vine has also, from the force of example, attracted attention of late years, particularly in the neighbourhoods of Camden and the Hunter. Other means of wealth within the reach of the farming class, to which attention has from time to time been drawn, have been neglected.

The growth of COTTON is one of these. It has been demonstrated, not only by articles in the newspapers, and by speeches in the Legislative Council, but by actual experiment, that cotton of the finest quality may be raised here at such a rate as to yield a fair profit to the grower. But, notwithstanding these demonstrations, and even the offer of small premiums by our legislature for the best specimens, cotton growing has as yet excited very little attention among those by whom it could be entered upon with the greatest advantage to themselves and to the community. Cotton has well been termed "the poor man's fleece." Commanding a ready sale and good prices, it may be raised without any outlay of capital beyond the means of the poorer class of cultivators, and without any demand for skill but such as may be readily acquired by persons of the most ordinary capacity.

The varieties of the cotton plant which have been found most valuable and productive in America have answered equally well in corresponding situations here; very superior samples of sea island cotton have been occasionally exhibited at the periodical shows of the Horticultural Society, and some which have been sent to England have elicited highly favourable opinions from the best judges of the article. Many of the soils of this colony, and especially the black sands, have been found peculiarly adapted to the growth of cotton. The times of planting and gathering the crops are also most favourable to the farmer; the former being just before the spring rains in October, and the latter about March. He may easily so arrange, therefore, as that the growth of cotton shall not interfere in the slightest degree with his grain producing operations. This branch of industry has also two other advantages. First, the greater portion of the labour which it entails is such as can be performed as well by women and children as by men, and perhaps better, thus furnishing remunerative employment for the husbandman's family. Secondly, the cotton plants will flourish and yield good crops in the driest seasons.

Much depends upon the quality of the seed, but seed of the finest quality can be procured gratuitously from Mr. S. A. Donaldson, of Sydney, who, both as a member of the Legislature and as a merchant, has laboured strenuously to call the attention of the colonists to the great importance of this species of production, Mr. Donaldson makes it a condition that those taking the seed shall render an account of its treatment and its productiveness; the object being to gather practical information, with a view to the benefit of the growers generally,

The cotton seeds have to be separated from the filaments, or wool, by passing the latter through a simple machine, called a gin, consisting of two small rollers set close together, like the flattening machines used by jewellers. A gin, wherewith some forty or fifty pounds of cotton may be cleaned in a day by one person, can be made in Sydney for two or three pounds; but if once the growth of cotton becomes general, machines worked by steam power will speedily be established here as in America, whereby cotton will be cleaned as corn is ground, either for a fixed charge, or for payment in "multure," and certainly at an infinitely cheaper rate than the work can be performed by hand.

By a statement in a Sydney paper, which has been quoted and adopted by Mr. Gardiner in his pamphlet, as a fair and reasonable guide, it would appear that an English acre planted in cotton would yield just cent. per cent. upon the outlay; the expenses being estimated at

£15, and the yield (300 lbs. of cotton at 9d per lb.) at £30. This, too, is reckoning upon a rental of two pounds for the acre, and all the inconveniences ot a small establishment.

The Sugar Cane has been found by actual experiment to thrive well, not only in the northern regions of the territory, such as Moreton Bay, but in districts much further south. Single specimens of cane have been brought to great perfection even in Sydney and its vicinity, and a few canes may be seen in the Government Gardens. The climate of this part of the colony, however, is not sufficiently warm throughout the entire year to admit of cane planting on a more extended scale.

There are a great many known varieties of the sugar cane, and it is by no means improbable that others may be discovered, on a more extended exploration of the Polynesian Islands, on most of which the cane is indigenous. The Tahitian variety, which is readily procurable, has long been celebrated among planters as one yielding sugar of a superior quality. Probably it would be the sort best adapted to this colony. But we have as yet no experience to guide us, and experience is the only safe test in such matters. One fact is worth fifty theories, however plausible.

The cane thrives best in strong and moist soils, attaining its largest size and yielding its finest juices when grown upon land of this description. A mixture of clay and sand has

has been found to produce crops of peculiar excellence, both as to quantity and quality. The next best description of soil is the rich black mould on the banks of rivers. On mere sandy lands the cane will not grow in any degree of perfection, unless by the aid of constant irrigation. It is raised in two ways; from slips and from suckers. The latter, technically called rattoons, produce the best juice, and although the *quantity* of juice is less under this system, still, as it entails less labour, it is frequently if not generally, preferred.

Sugar planting, properly so called, is an operation above all others requiring large investments of capital to ensure success. The mere culture is simple enough, and requires no more costly implements than such as are necessary for any other species of husbandry; but the processes of expressing the juice, of boiling, and of distilling, require machinery and erections of an expensive character. The juice of the cane may no doubt be expressed in a mill of simple structure, and may be boiled in common iron pots. The still also may be a very inexpensive sort of affair. But a planter carrying on business in this way would have no chance whatever of competing with the importers, especially if he had to employ labour at a high rate. The small farmer, therefore, could scarcely grow the sugar cane with profit, unless perhaps by disposing of the cane juice for distillation, or sending the canes to the mill of a capitalist. In the former case a simple and cheaply constructed kind of mill would probably suffice.

The sugar mill consists of three rollers set horizontally, one above and two below; the former is made to revolve by the application of steam, water, or animal power, and a cog wheel at its extremity turns the other two. The canes passing between these rollers are crushed, and the juice falls into a receiver at the bottom. In old mills the rollers were set perpendicularly, being put in motion by cogs from the middle roller, to which the "first mover" was directly applied. Mills upon this principle, and of exceedingly simple structure, working with hand bars like a ship's capstan, have been introduced at many of the South Sea Islands; but the horizontal mill is so much easier fed, and so much better in every respect, that even when this extreme simplicity of structure is desirable, it would be found the most advantageous. And it may be constructed with equal facility. The only addition required is a bevel wheel to change the direction of the motion. The best mill for the Australian grower, where simplicity and cheapness are the main objects, would be one of this nature, to be worked by a horse or bullock. A slight fall of water, where such can be had, is peculiarly applicable as a moving power for a horizontal sugar mill. The principle of the windmill is occasionally applied, but it is scarcely suitable on account of its uncertainty; for when the canes have once been cut they require to be passed through the mill as rapidly as possible, in order to prevent fermentation.

In sugar growing countries it is only the refuse which is subjected to the action of the still, the average rates of produce being usually from sixty to seventy gallons of rum to every hogshead (16 cwt.) of sugar. In Java the produce of sugar to the acre has been estimated * at averages of from 1285 lbs. to 1815 lbs. In Sumatra and many other islands of the Indian archipelago, where the cane is extensively cultivated, its juice is evaporated only to the consistence of a syrup.

There are many other branches of productive industry coming properly within the sphere of an agriculturist's operations, which are as yet untried or nearly so, although some of them could scarcely fail to be very profitable. The growth of the olive has been found to present but little attraction, owing to the time which must elapse before the plantation would arrive at maturity, but the breeding of the SILK WORM offers no objection of this nature. There is no delay here, but a certain annual produce obtained with little or no outlay, and with only such an application of industry as a settler's or labourer's children would readily apply as a matter of amusement. The chief cause of inattention to this branch of production has been the failure of an experimental plantation which some of the leading colonists

* Vide Porter on the sugar-cane.

established a few years since. But this failure ought not to have any influence when it is recollected at the same time how successful private experimentalists have been. Mr. Foster (formerly proprietor of the *Australian* newspaper), and many others, have produced silk of very superior quality and have ascertained beyond question the practicability of this being done profitably. In such a country as this, establishments for producing silk alone would not perhaps be found to pay very well, but the settler might find great advantage in turning his attention to it in connexion with his other pursuits. The production of raw silk, is one of those employments which might be introduced with peculiar advantage into the pastoral districts of the interior, if the regulations would admit of it. It would be found a most powerful aid in getting rid of the barbarism which even yet prevails in many of those districts by the employment of men only and by the consequent regard of women and children as "incumbrances."

Many of the difficulties in the way of the agriculturists, are such as may be overcome with a little attention and industry. Even the greatest of all, drought, may often be thus successfully grappled with. The bad effects of dryness, may at all times be greatly counteracted by the judicious application of manures. But in many situations, large reservoirs of water might be made by taking advantage of the natural formation of the ground, and erecting a small embankment or two. The fall of rain during the year is very great. In the neighbourhood of Sydney it amounts to above forty inches. It is clear, therefore, that if the water flowing over the surface and serving only to increase the destructive power of the floods, could be secured in tanks, a very copious supply would be ensured. In the neighbourhood of running streams or large water holes (ponds), IRRIGATION is simple enough, although but little practised. Where there is anything like a current a small water-wheel, fitted with float boards and moved simply by the velocity of the stream, may be used with advantage, but generally speaking a small windmill turning a simple crank, and thus working an ordinary pump, will be found best. The water should be pumped into a reservoir, and from thence it may be spread through a farm by means of wooden gutters. The latter are readily formed by nailing together at right angles two pieces of sawed stuff, or even of the split stuff ordinarily used for fencing. Water may be raised to any height for the purposes of irrigation by the formation of additional reservoirs, and the construction of additional windmills.

MANURES are far more numerous than most persons imagine. When manure is spoken of, the produce of stables, cow-houses, &c., is suggested to the mind of the hearer. But there is scarcely anything in nature—certainly nothing

among the apparently useless rubbish cast out
from the abodes of men and animals, &c., which is
not eminently useful as manure for some
kind of land or another. An admixture of
soil is often more advantageous than manuring
to any extent would be : as for instance—in
the admixture of dry sand and peat, or bog
soil. Many of the advantages of manuring
may likewise be derived from a judicious
rotation of crops.

HORTICULTURE.

We now come to the subject of horticulture,
and would remark that in very young communities, though from old associations at first the
habits and manners of the parent country are
imitated as closely as possible, yet, as they
advance in self-dependence, as they become
wrapped up in their own interests, these
associations gradually and silently die away, at
least such of them as may be uncongenial to the
circumstances in which the colonist is placed.

Such has been the case to some extent with
regard to horticulture. Even at this remote
date, in the oldest parts of the city—on the
Rocks, in the middle of the most crowded business thoroughfares the attentive observer may
trace the lingering signs of gardens which have
long since passed away. Some creeping
parasite giving verdure and freshness to a
bonded store, some green and weeping willow
shedding its rural influences over the pump

and brew-house of the confined yard of a Sydney mansion—dwarf pines, whose stunted growth is venerable from the affection that leaves them standing amidst the smoke of factories or the enclosed courts of official buildings, in the vain hope that they may yet rear their lofty heads in grand and matured pride — all these are the remnant of that imitative spirit of the first settlers of the colony here, who would, as far as they were able, have carried out the garden-loving propensities of their ancestors.

The rapid growth of the city, the absorbing nature of the pursuits of its inhabitants, have destroyed, or rather worn away the English tastes which at first prevailed, and although even now, bounded on one side by the largest and busiest of our wharves, and on the other by the greatest business street of the city, a large garden exists and flourishes—it is the oasis in the desert—its companions in the old days of the colony have vanished, and are now the sites of the homes of the citizens, or the marts of trade.

We regret to see a more decided and more unamiable symptom of the indifference to gardening which prevails in this colony. We mean that which is exhibited in the neglect of the fine, large, and originally well laid out gardens which surround many of our large country mansions. There are some splendid exceptions no doubt, where not only is the strictest attention and most liberal expenditure devoted to this greatest ornament of a gentleman's estate, but in which everything that is rich and rare in the science of botany is eagerly collected and carefully cultivated. But round many of the beautiful country seats which adorn the interior of the colony, the gardens are desolate places, weeds and flowers, shrubs and fruit trees, growing together in un-pruned and untended luxuriance.

The neglect may in many instances perhaps be accounted for, by the decay of the fortunes of the original owners of these mansions. They were ruined by the terrible financial convulsions of the years 1842 and 1843. Their property passed through the insolvent court into new hands—in many instances into the hands of men of entirely different tastes and different education—men whose souls were in mere material interests and physical enjoy-ments, and who had no time and no thought to give to the rural and the picturesque.

In the City of Sydney, from the nature of the soil, and from the crowded design on which the Government by their sale of the land, have thought fit to cover it with houses, it is im-possible that gardens should exist ; but the beautiful Botanic Gardens sloping down to the waters of the harbour, and almost adjoining the busy Circular Quay, give a proof of what might under a more enlightened and more liberal state of things have been done to have crowned this great city in a manner worthy of her royal dignity, as Queen of the Pacific.

In the suburbs of the city, at Woolloomoolloo, Newtown, and the Glebe, there are many large and highly cultivated gardens ; and accordingly these suburbs are sought after as the dwelling places of the opulent classes. It is an unfortunate thing that there is but little opportunity of affording the working classes — the labourer and the mechanic—the delightful and beneficial relaxation of gardening. As we have said the land in the city is entirely devoted to building, and the suburbs, where land attached to a house of sufficient extent could be rented at a moderate rate, are too distant to allow the poor man to follow his ordinary avocations. It has been suggested, that large breadths of land suitable for gardens, (of which there are many in the immediate neighbourhood of the city,) should be bought up, and Garden Societies, on the principle of Building Societies, be established. The land would be divided into a number of small allotments, each being as much as one man would be able to cultivate in his leisure hours, and these little gardens could be let on such a system, at an almost nominal rent. Such a plan will we hope yet be carried out, as we should certainly like to see the luxury of rearing one's own vegetables, and of pulling one's own flowers, less exclusively enjoyed than it is at present.

In the country towns of the colony, where there is abundance of land fit for cultivation, almost every hut and cottage has its patch of garden ground, but even there for the most part, (if we except Parramatta,) very little care is taken to make it either useful, ornamental, or beneficial. A few vegetables —an old peach tree—and some flowers, which will bloom in spite of neglect, shew rather what the garden was, and what it might be made, than that it is at all prized by the possessor.

These are bad syptoms, and we hope that a reformation will soon take place, and we are led to anticipate that it will. There was formerly a very great pride taken by the inhabitants of the colony in the floral productions of the colony, and we are inclined to think this feeling is reviving. During its slumber, however, many scientific men of taste and wealth have been busy cultivating, and our flower shows, though for the most part meagre in the collections they exhibit, always contain specimens of beautiful and curious plants which would do honor to any European exhibition.

The Botanic Gardens of Sydney are sufficiently indicative of the capabilities of the soil and climate of New South Wales for the pursuits of holticulture. There you have collected the shrubs and flowers of almost every country; such as the English oak and the Norway pine — dwarfed in their dimensions yet still flourishing in their native verdure—while the violet, the primrose, the polyanthus are even more bashful than at home; and the little snowdrop is a wonder, which chance only enables the skilful florist to exhibit.

But to make even a small garden gay and beautiful is, in this colony, a very easy task. Flowers of easy culture and which best set off a garden, bloom all the year round. Roses, both white and red, are always in flower. Verbenas, petunias, mignionette, sylvias and the whole tribe of Labiates, orchids, amaryillds, irids, geraniums, dahlias, and fuchsias are almost continually blooming. Camellias, azaleas, bignonias, gardenias, and magnolias grow out of doors in great richness and beauty. In shrubs there is even still greater variety ; for joined to all the best European varieties we have a large collection of charming ornaments to the garden selected from the wild bush of this continent and the surrounding islands.

In trees the whole tribe of Fabaceæ, including many indigenous specimens of Acacia, Mimosa, and Erythrina grown with surprising rapidity, and with their glowing colours and graceful verdure beautify our shruberries. Our Moreton Bay and Norfolk Island pines cannot be appreciated by those who have not seen the grace and beauty to which they attain in this colony. The Moreton Bay chestnut (costasnospernum) is a beautiful tree—and the whole Ficus tribe grow with a grandeur of leaf almost unequalled in any other part of the world. To attempt to enter into a detailed list of the various genera of the flowers, shrubs, and trees, which would freely flourish here, would be tedious and

out of place in a work which makes no pretension to scientific disquisition ; but we think
we have enumerated sufficiently the
distinguishing ornaments of our gardens, to
show that floriculture, and horticulture, may be
pursued here to the pleasure, instruction, and
benefit of all who have a taste for its delightful fascinations.   Nor are the more useful
adjuncts of the garden wanting.   Vegetables
with but little care, may be cultivated with the
greatest ease, of the finest quality, and in the
richest abundance.   We have potatoes,
cabbages,   peas,   pumpkins,   beans   of
all   sorts,   brocoli,   cauliflowers,   vegetable   marrows,   lettuces,   radishes,   arti-
chokes, parsnips, carrots, turnips, spinach, sea
kale,   celery,   cresses,   cucumbers,   squash,
onions, leeks, in fact every imaginable variety
of esculent in a perfection, that is not surpassed
in any part of the world.

In fruit we have an immense variety of
apples, including all the most valued kinds
both for the table and the kitchen. Pears
grow fine and in greater luxuriance here than
we ever saw them in other parts of the world.
The Bergamot, Beaurrè, and Marie Louise
pears carefully grown in this colony, would
furnish a desert for an emperor. We have med-
lars, loquats, almonds, apricots, peaches, quinces
nectarines, plums, oranges, cherries, lemons
limes, citrons, guavas, shadocks, figs, mulberries,
nuts, bananas, cheromoyers, walnuts, passion
fruit, grapes, pine apples, strawberries, melons,

pomegranates, and all these in no stinted store, but in great profusion. Englishmen would be astounded if they knew the enormous quantities of apricots, peaches, nectarines, pears, and loquats, which annually rot and perish under our trees. And this abundance is, moreover, the result of the richness of the soil and climate, Art and skilful culture do but little. Trees are left unpruned; crops of the most cumbrous luxuriance are allowed to destroy the healthful energies of the plant, which ought to be husbanded with a prudent hand.

It is to this cause that is to be attributed the inferior quality which is talked of by some unthinking persons, as the characteristic of Australian fruits. It is not the character of the fruit that is bad, it is the culture, that is bad. The Australian peach, nectarine, apricot, pear, or pine-apple, cultivated with equal skill and care, is equal in quality to the same fruit grown in any part of the world. It is attention and skill that is wanted, and to obtain this a taste for gardening must be more generally diffused through the country. To the gratification of such a taste the parterre, the kitchen garden, and the orchard alike offer abundant opportunity, and rich reward.

THE VINE AND ITS PRODUCTS.

The culture of the Vine, although it has not yet attracted so much attention throughout the colony as could be wished, has nevertheless become pretty general.

Many enterprising men among the early settlers were convinced that Australia was peculiarly suited, in soil and climate, to become a great wine-producing country. But those who first turned their attention to this branch of industry laboured under great disadvantages. It was found not only difficult, but almost impossible, to get out *genuine* collections of vines. The European vignerons palmed off cuttings of the most worthless kinds as the productions of the finest. The fraud was one which could not be detected for a considerable period, and the cuttings were to be planted a long way off. The temptation to palm off mere rubbish was consequently very strong. But, perhaps, the greatest mischief which was done in this way proceeded, not from fraud or carelessness on the part of the European vigneron, but from the dishonesty of parties with whom it was necessary to deposit the collections while they awaited shipment. It was so easy for these people to abstract the valuable sorts from a collection, and to substitute some of their own worthless cuttings, that in very many cases they could not resist the temptation. Perseverance, however, conquered this, as well as other difficulties, and cuttings or rooted plants, of all the best kinds, may now be procured from colonial vineyards at cheap rates.

Although the more intelligent settlers perceived at once the advantages to be derived from vine culture, and, seeing this, turned their attention to it, more or less, as a collateral pursuit; the farmers, as a body, could not be brought to appreciate these advantages. It was not until vineyards of some magnitude were in full and prosperous operation, and their own senses of seeing and tasting convinced them of the practicability of wine-making, that the vineyard began to make its appearance as one of the adjuncts of a " small farm."

But even at the present time vineyards are not so general a feature of the settler's holding as they ought to be. In the neighbourhood of Camden, on the banks of the Hunter, and in a few other situations where there are near at hand the examples of the higher class of agriculturalists to act as a spur, vineyards, small or large, are everywhere to be met with; but in other parts of the country they are almost unknown.

The progress of this branch of industry will be best shewn by a glance at the statistical returns of the last seven years. In 1845 there were 611 acres of vineyard under cultivation throughout the colony, producing 54,996 gallons of wine, and 1433 gallons of brandy. In 1846 the quantity of land under vine was 749 acres, and its production was 52,337 gallons of wine, and 1383 gallons of brandy. In 1847 there were 899 acres of vineyard, producing 54,035 gallons of wine, and 1402 gallons of brandy. In 1848 there were 887 acres of vineyard, producing 97,300 gallons of wine, and

1163 gallons of brandy. In 1849 there were 963 acres of vineyard, producing 95,843 gallons of wine, and 1266 gallons of brandy. In 1850 there were 1069¾ acres of vineyard, producing 111,085 gallons of wine, and 1958 gallons of brandy. And in 1851 there were 1060¼ acres of vineyard, producing 84,843 gallons of wine, and 1641 gallons of brandy.

There is at present no means of judging with any degree of certainty as to how far the production of colonial wines will be affected by the progress of the gold discoveries. The difference between 1851 and the preceding year was, it will be perceived, but 9½ acres, and this slight variation proves nothing definite. In all probability there will not at present be either an increase or a decrease worthy of note; but as population becomes more dense throughout the interior, and the necessity for enlarging the means of remunerative employment becomes more obvious, vineyards will spring up with greater rapidity than heretofore.

The vine-grower is allowed, by a colonial statute, to distil brandy from grapes the produce of his own vineyard, without being subjected to the imposts placed upon other kinds of distillation. This provision, as will be seen from the returns already quoted, has not been taken advantage of to such an extent as might have been anticipated; and the brandies which *have* been made, although peculiarly remarkable for strength, have been for the most part of inferior flavor. A few samples of very superior spirit have, however, been produced; and the general inferiority has, probably, arisen from a practice which has grown up of distilling from refuse only, instead of cultivating certain kinds of grape expressly with a view to the manufacture of spirit.

The Australian wines are many of them very fine, particularly those manufactured of late years. In the first instance most of the growers turned their attention rather to quantity than quality, and some very inferior wines were the result. Latterly, the example of the principle vignerons, the good effect of co-operation, the spirit of emulation, kindled by the periodi, cal exhibitions of the Vineyard Associations and the favourable reception which some of our best wines have met in other lands, have caused the production of a really good wine to be generally regarded as of more importance than the preparation of inferior stuff in large quantities.

The wines of this country, like those of every separate region where the vine flourishes, have a character peculiarly their own. Many which have been sold under the denominations of clarets, &c., resemble indeed the European wines of the same name; but all of them have, more or less, a flavor and bouquet which is peculiarly Australian. By some this has been regarded as a defect, but as the flavor and bouquet are both agreeable, (although peculiar and indescribable,) they are more likely to prove a recommendation in Foreign Markets. Many of the wines made in latter years want but age to develop their true qualities in order to obtain a reputation equal to those of the most favoured wine-producing countries of Europe. The general character of our wines, as a production, will also no doubt improve as the vineyards themselves get older, and the vignerons acquire more experience.

The quantity of wine manufactured during the past year affords but little guide as to the quantity in the market, for much of the new wine is of course stored to acquire age. But the produce of the vintage of 1851 being less than that of any year since 1847, it may be fairly assumed that the quantity of wine actually consumed at home or abroad, during the year, was not *less* than the quantity produced. Now the quantity of Colonial wine exported in this period was but 3050 gallons, which gives 81,793 gallons as the quantity consumed within the colony. As it is almost impossible for a colonist to purchase Colonial wines in small quantities for household use, and as Colonial wines are very seldom to be met with (in their true character at least) at houses of entertainment, the obvious conclusion is that they must be sold under " false colors" as the wines of France or Germany. The true John Bull partiality for things foreign is as strong in Sydney as in London; and as the better kinds of Australian wines are rather dear, the retailers re-christen their commodities to suit the whims of their customers. This practice however, is really injurious to the vigneron. He has not the advantage of that criticism upon his produce to which, and to its influence, he is as much entitled as to the money value of the wine. And even the latter is diminished. The colonists as a body are victimised, and those who would prefer the known and really excellent wines of our own growth, to the equivocal and often inferior wines which are imported, have no means of procuring the former, unless by purchasing largely from the growers. The writer of this paper has frequently during the last five or six years endeavoured to call the attention of the vine growers to this fact, but without effect. Recently, however, the Chief Justice having pointed out the evil, and suggested to the New South Wales Vineyard Association the propriety of establishing some kind of depôt where colonial wines may be procured in their true character, that body has appointed a sub-committee to take the subject into consideration.

One error into which the wine growers have fallen, has been a pertinacious adherence to the spirit of imitation. All, or most of our wines, are "claret," "Burgundy," &c., &c., according to their resemblance, either real or fancied, to the foreign wines of the same names. This may be all very well in dealing with the inferior productions which have no decided character or merits of their own ; but the superior wines really lose much by this system. Call a

z

wine sherry, Burgundy, Constantia, or any other name chosen in this spirit of imitation, and a comparison with the foreign wine of the same name is challenged. Judged by this standard it will, in all probability, be pronounced inferior ; but challenge for it a standing based upon its own merits call it by the name of the estate on which it was produced, or by any other *original* designation—and its true value will be appreciated.

Australian wine will not come into general consumption until the small farmers, as a class, thoroughly awakened to their own interests, become vine growers ; each according to his means. Vignerons, possessed of capital, naturally turn their attention to the production of a superior and high priced article. For cheap light wines for ordinary consumption, we must look to the man who, with his own hands and the aid of his family, cultivates a small vineyard with a view to the production of as large a quantity of wine as possible for immediate sale. From the Gouais grape, which grows and bears admirably in this climate a well-flavored light wine has been made, which, if manufactured more extensively, would, with other wines of the same class, be sold with good profit to the growers at a sufficiently low rate to come into general consumption, and to drive out of the market much of the adulterated and pernicious yet costly stuff, now retailed in the character of spirits and malt liquors. A light wholesome wine, retailed at about 3s. per gallon, would meet with ready sale. Most of the Australian wines at present in the market are of a higher quality, and not procurable in small quantities under twice or thrice that price.

The small farmer, desirous of planting vines can do so with very little outlay. Cuttings of any kind, ready for planting, can be procured for 5s. to £2 per thousand, and the labour which is entailed by a small vineyard, he and his family may easily get through, without materially interfering with their other avocations. What is chiefly wanted at present is a plain and cheap, but comprehensive manual of instructions. Several able works of this kind have been written, but they are for the most part out of print. The gentleman who produced one of the best of these works, however, as it is reported, promised to supply the existing deficiency before long.

One of the greatest difficulties which the manufacturer of the Australian wine has had to contend against of late, has been that of procuring bottles, and they now have under consideration the propriety of establishing a bottle factory. This however is a difficulty which would not affect the producers of light cheap wines for immediate consumption, as these wines would need no bottling

PART V.

Pastoral Pursuits.

THE pursuit by which the progress of the Colony of New South Wales (including the district of Port Phillip) to wealth and importance has been most aided, has been undoubtedly that of sheep farming.

In the early days of the colony industry among the free classes and their servants was limited to the production of the necessaries of life, while the convict population under the restraint of the government were employed in those public works which are so eminently necessary to the settlement of all new and wild countries. Houses for the governor and his officers, barracks for the prisoners and the soldiers who were sent to guard them, had to be built. Land for the site of a township had to be cleared and laid out, and to these works for a number of years the labours of the early colonists were mainly directed. As, however, the settlers became comfortable and prosperous in their wild and adopted country, the spirit of British enterprise began to incite them to bolder and more aspiring views. They looked round upon the land and saw that it was good. They built houses, and planted gardens and vineyards. They looked on the broad waters spread open before them, seeming to invite them to come and take the wealth that lay beneath their glittering waves; and the colonists were not deaf to the call. The fisheries were the first field of Australian commercial enterprise; oil, whalebone, tortoiseshell, and seal skins, were the first Australian articles of export.

But at a very early period of the settlement of the colony, it was found that the natural grasses which grew abundantly on the plains of New South Wales were admirably adapted to the grazing of sheep and cattle. Flocks and herds increased with great rapidity, and seemed to point out that the national pursuit of the colony, for a long period, in fact till the whole land should be replenished and subdued by the footsteps of civilisation and settlement, would be wool-growing.

Of course, as in all other similar cases, it required some penetrating and master mind to seize upon the advantages thus opened to the future—to look with far-seeing eye into the coming time, and with firm faith, and strong and unswerving arm, to work out the event, the shadow of which had been cast before.

Such a mind was not wanting, even at the very outset of the colony. In the year 1793, only six years after the settlement of the colony, Captain John Macarthur, one of the earliest and most active settlers in New South Wales, was struck, from his experience in Europe and the nature of the grasses here, with the conviction that the Merino sheep, so justly celebrated for the quality of its wool in the markets of England, could be propagated to an enormous extent here. Determined to work this conviction out, Captain Macarthur two years after obtained a Merino ram and two ewes, which had been brought from the Cape, where they had been sent by the Dutch government. With these " patriarchs of the Australian flocks," Captain Macarthur commenced a series of experiments, crossing the common coarse woolled sheep of his flock with the Merinos, and at the expiration of four years his stock of 70 animals was increased to 4000.

Up to the present time, in almost every crisis in which the good or evil in the destinies of Australia have seemed to tremble on the scale, external circumstances have not only secured the preponderance of the good, but the development of what at first served to tend only to individual prosperity, has secured the permanent accumulation of great national wealth.

So it was with regard to the wool of Australia; the quality and abundance of the natural grasses, the adaptation of the climate, the unbounded plains would, perhaps, under any circumstances have induced the occupation of this country by a nomadic race—but it would have been a race such as ever existed in most other pastoral countries, wild, ignorant, and semi-civlized, had it not been that coincidently with the growth of sheep farming, other more active energies were brought into play.

In the year 1803, Mr. Macarthur visited England, and having exhibited samples of the wool from his improved flocks to several mercantile gentlemen, he was summoned before the Privy Council to give information on the subject. The growing importance of the woollen trade of England, the enormous increase in the manufacture and consumption of woollen goods, and the entire dependence for the supply of the finer wools under which Great Britain was placed to Germany and Spain, had enlisted the serious consideration not only of the mercantile portion of the English world but also of the government of the empire. Under these circumstances it may well be imagined that the Privy Council were favourably disposed to hear Captain Macarthur propound his theory for rendering England independent of foreign countries for the supply of fine wools.

There was, moreover, something peculiarly encouraging and interesting in the hope that a settlement which, in its origin and conception, had very little in common with the ordinary work of colonization, properly so called, but which was destined merely as the receptacle of Britain's penal offenders, should become, in a commercial point of view, so desirable an appanage of the British Crown.

Even in those old days there was something

harsh and revolting in the idea of a mere settlement of convicts; there were some compunctious visitings of conscience perhaps, as to the right and justice of planting hordes of abandoned, reckless, and hardened men on distant shores, without any pursuit to elevate them from their state of degradation by the hopes and aspirations . it might encourage. Even in the good old times, " when George the third was King," and Botany Bay was as dark a blot on the page of British history as the cities of the plain were on that of Palestine, there was something pleasing in the prospect of the amelioration of the title " of one huge gaol" into that of " one great sheep walk" - the picturesque of the shepherd's crook, and the music of the shepherd's pipe, would at least furnish some set-off to the disgrace of the prisoner's manacle and the sound of the scourger's lash. We do not say that these ideas were very vividly impressed on the minds of her Majesty's government of that day, but they might have exercised some sort of secret influence on the spirit of encouragement with which Captain Macarthur's proposal was met. Certainly, the " Australian Arcady" has not been such as to fulfil such dreamy illusions if they were ever indulged.

At the period at which Mr. Macarthur commenced his experiments, the sheep in the colony were bred from stock imported almost exclusively from the Cape of Good Hope and

Bengal. In the first twelve years of the colony's existence only 304 sheep were imported altogether, but at the end of that period the stock in the colony was 6757. An enormous increase, considering that during this period they were bred almost exclusively for food.

Captain Macarthur having received the encouragement of the Privy Council, purchased from the Merino flock of George III. two ewes and three rams, with which he returned to New South Wales, and from that time devoted his attention to sheep-farming, with a view mainly to the growth of wool. For several years he continued to import from the best European flocks, until at last, it having been indisputably proved, that an almost illimitable supply of fine wool could be produced in Australia, enterprise was rapidly devoted to that pursuit. Men of capital and of good family, retired officers of the army and navy, anxious for retirement, and unable to bear the expense of respectable idleness in England, younger sons who having received their thrifty portion were expected thenceforth to provide for themselves, allured by the prospect of grants of land, assigned servants, immense returns in the produce of their flocks, and a life of easy independence, flocked to the shores of the new Arcadia, and from that period the growth of wool became and has continued the leading industrial pursuit of these colonies.

We have said that other energies were called forth at the same period which prevented the

z 4

inhabitants of this colony from sinking to the level of the nomadic races which exist in most other pastoral countries. It is proper here that we should explain what those energies were, and the circumstances which brought them into play. In pastoral countries, generally, the inhabitants are poor, they tend sheep for the mere obtainance of a livelihood; they are countries which possess little or no money capital, and in which there are little or no money exchanges; they exchange wool and sheepskins, as the North Americans do furs and feathers, for articles of food and clothing, and the implements of war and the chase. In New South Wales, though the natural capabilities of the soil and climate for the purpose of wool-growing are unequalled in the whole world, wool-growing was resorted to, not in consequence of the natural fitness and adaptation of things, but as a commercial enterprise, the success of which was secured by two concurrent circumstances : first, by the increasing want of an article in England, arising out of advancing civilization and the increase of population; and second, the ability of this colony to supply that want to an indefinite extent, from the almost boundless expanse of its unpeopled plains. The pastoral element and the commercial element were thus happily blended together, the former invigorating the latter in such a way as to make it effective in reducing the colony gradually to a state of settlement and civilization.

There was no absolute necessity for resorting to this pursuit; the cultivation of the land and the rearing of stock, poultry, the planting of orchards and vineyards, were of themselves sufficient to furnish the limited number of early settlers with the comforts and luxuries of life, and even to accumulate wealth, because there was a very large money expenditure going on in the colony by the commissariat for convicts and military purposes. But, had it not been for the growth of wool, or something in its place, the colony must have remained for ever a convict colony, shut out for ever from those free, political, social, and educational institutions which constitute the glory of a state. It was to redeem the colony from this state of degradation that the physical adaptation of the country to the growth of wool was revealed to us, and well has the pastoral enterprise thus excited fulfilled its mission. Thus, as soon as the success of the first efforts became apparent, its effect on the commerce of the country was decisive. With the spread of flocks over the vast interior, arose the stores and wharves, which formed the nucleus of the city of Sydney. Ships thronged into our harbour, richly freighted with merchandise; Banks and merchants were established to advance on wool and to ship it to the hungry market 16,000 miles away; the sheep farmer was engaged in a sort of mixed pursuit, half pastoral and half commercial, he was growing wool—but he was growing

In this year, 1845, the amount of license fees collected was £32,031.

The main points with which the squatters were dissatisfied on these regulations were, that they gave them no fixity of tenure, no right of pre-emption, and no compensation for improvements made on the Crown lands.

They contended that their occupation ought to be in some degree permanent. That the squatter ought not to be ousted from a station to the ruin of his property, because some person chose to purchase from the Crown the choice bit of land, which perhaps gave value to all the pastoral acres which surrounded it. They urged, if at the claim of intending purchasers land was put up for sale, the occupying squatter should have the option of buying it at the upset price ; and they demanded, that if their stations were taken from them they should have full value for all improvements made upon them. These demands were resisted by the Local Government, and a feeling of very considerable bitterness was thus engendered ; and it is a matter of very considerable doubt whether this bitterness, together with the self-interest of one of the contending parties, did not prevent the ultimate settlement of the question by the Imperial Government, from being based on wise policy and correct principles. It is quite certain that at the present time, the feeling throughout the Colony that the squatters have attained privileges which are unjust and which are dangerous to the liberties of the country, is rapidly gaining strength.

An agrarian spirit of discontent has been evinced at the locking up immense districts in the most fertile parts of the colony from settlement or cultivation ; it is exhibited by the lower classes, who complain they are thus prohibited from settling on small farms and country homesteads of their own ; still more, reflective men incline very much to the opinion that by the undue encouragement given to sheep farming, the industrial and productive energies of the country have been materially crippled.

In these papers, however, it would be out of place to discuss a question of this nature, we therefore proceed to point out the principal features of the regulations established under an order of Council, and under which squatting is at present carried on.

The order in Council was dated 9th March, 1847, and came into operation on the 7th October of that year ; and under it the lands of the colony were divided into three classes—the settled, the intermediate, and the unsettled districts. The settled districts in the colony of New South Wales comprise the whole of the nineteen counties, the counties of Stanley and Macquarie, the towns in the country districts with the lands immediately adjacent, all the land within three miles of the sea, and the lands at the head and along the banks of some principal rivers.

The intermediate districts in New South Wales comprehend the county of Auckland, Gipps Land, and some other partially settled districts.

The unsettled districts comprise all the remaining lands of the colony.

In the unsettled districts occupation leases are given for 14 years, with the right to cultivate for the consumption of the establishment of the lessee, and no further; the amount of rent being ten pounds per annum for the estimated capability of the run to carry 4000 sheep or an equivalent number of cattle; the capability of the run to be determined by two valuers, one appointed by the Commissioner of the district, and one by the occupier. During the lease the land can be sold only to the occupant. The lease may be renewed for the whole run if no portion is sold, or for any portion of the run, provided that one-fourth of the whole remains unsold.

In the leases there are reservations for public purposes, and conditions for the payment of rent, &c., punishable by the forfeiture of the run in case of non-observance.

In the intermediate districts, the leases are confined to 8 years, it being, however, a condition that at the end of every successive year from the date of the lease, the Governor may, by giving 60 days' previous notice, offer for sale the whole or any part of the lands on the said run.

In the settled districts the leases are given from year to year only.

This, then, is the position, politically speaking, in which the pastoral districts now stand ; but we may add that it was only under the constitutional act of 1850, that the population outside the boundaries were allowed the elective franchise. At present, however, the squatting districts have been erected, under certain combinations, into electoral districts, and exercise very considerable influence in the Legislature of the country.

We now proceed to examine what have been the results of the workings of these successive systems.

In the year 1810, twenty-two years after the establishment of the country, the sheep of the colony were 25,888 head, and the cattle 12,442. In the year 1821, the number of sheep had increased to 119,777 ; in 1828, it was 563,691 ; in 1834, it reached one million ; in 1843, the number of sheep was 3,452,539 ; in 1844, 3,743,732 ; in 1845, 4,409,504 ; in 1846, 4,909,819 ; in 1847, 5,673,266 ; in 1848, 6,530,542 ; in 1849, 6,784,494 ; in 1850, 7,092,209 ; in 1851, 7,396,895. In 1837, the export of wool was 4,273,715 lbs. ; in 1840, it was 7,668,960 lbs.; in 1845, it was 10,522,921 lbs. ; in 1850, it was 14,270,632 lbs.; in 1851, it was 15,268,473 lbs.

Whether therefore it be that the pasturage and climate of New South Wales is peculiarly favorable for the breeding of sheep, or whether it be from the peculiar system under which this pursuit has been carried on, there can be

of New South Wales *is*, in proportion to the number of its population, the largest meat consuming one in the world. At all events, it is the largest consuming community of beef and mutton, as there is little fish, and scarcely any game.

When then it is considered that the pastoral pursuits of the colony afford an export very nearly amounting to £6 per head for every man, woman, and child in the colony—that they supply in abundance, and at a very cheap rate, the second important element in the food of the country, and that they form, moreover, to such an enormous proportionate extent as we have described, the permanent and fixed capital of the country, it is difficult to rate their importance too highly, and it is certainly somewhat dangerous to interfere with interests so essential to the present prosperity of the country, and which from their magnitude must be so powerful and influential. Sorry indeed should we be to see the capital, labour, and enterprise, which has hitherto been—so prosperously to the country,— invested in these pursuits, and which has so largely fructified, either destroyed or depreciated.

But we cannot conceal from ourselves that the wool and grazing interests in their present state, impede in some degree the social progress of the country.

The policy of dispersion as opposed to concentration, though rendered almost inevitable under the natural circumstances of the country, can never be regarded as very favorable for the advancement of civilization and refinement ; and in the case of New South Wales, this has proved to be particularly the case. The class who in general, in civilized countries, are the promoters of material progress, have here, under the influence of self-interest, opposed it.

The formation of railroads, the establishment of manufactures, the encouragement of agriculture by the humble classes, have been discountenanced, because they would have absorbed the labour which was required for pastoral pursuits.

The gold discovery is however rapidly breaking up this spirit of monopoly, and though we trust the pastoral interests will ultimately escape from the injury its changes may bring, we do warmly anticipate that it will do more than any purely human efforts could have effected, to extend the sphere of industrial enterprise, and to advance the progress of moral, social, and intellectual refinement.

PART VI.

Commerce and Manufactures.

COMMERCE.

THERE are perhaps few communities in the world in which the mercantile character is more decidedly developed than in the colony of New South Wales.

Commerce indeed may be termed the genius of this growing dependency, and to any reflecting mind, having opportunities of observation, it must be evident that to commerce will it owe that place in the scale of nations which it is doubtless destined to attain.

That this should be the case is to a certain extent natural, while that this peculiar characteristic tendency should be so strikingly displayed is perhaps somewhat singular. Descended from a great commercial nation, it was to be expected that the habits and pursuits of the colony should resemble those of the parent state; but the circumstances of the former—its physical features, its capacity for production, and the nature of its products, all inclined to the supposition that if habits of trade were adopted they would exist only under a very changed and modified form.

This however has not turned out to be the case, at least to a very slight extent. Although, as we have shown in a former paper, the wealth of this colony has mainly depended on its production of wool, and it may therefore to that extent be termed a pastoral country, the manners and habits of the community are by no means such as we are accustomed to attribute to a pastoral people. In New South Wales there is all the vigorous energy, all the ardent enterprise, all the shrewd speculative spirit which are to be found amongst the most intelligent of commercial communities. While the true British genius is displayed in the breadth and design of the commercial fabric, there is almost an American cleverness and activity in the conduct of the details of trade. Alive to the fullest extent to the power and greatness which in these modern times attaches to the material wealth of communites, addicted to the pursuit of commerce,—as much from a restless spirit of excitement as by the desire of personal gain,—all the productive capabilities of the country have been nourished and fostered with the view of making them subservient to the commercial greatness of the colony.

It was this that engendered and encouraged the growth of wool in the colony, as the leading pursuit. It was the merchants, the bankers, the traders of the city of Sydney, who stimulated this enterprise, by investing their own funds largely in it, and by advancing means to others. Pastoral pursuits were not resorted to

in this colony as the means of subsistence, but
to furnish the materials of a trade. The great
reason why the increase in the production of
wool has been so large and so rapid has been
because the end to be obtained could be enlarged to an indefinite extent. It was to give
us a large export : it became to the mercantile
man the sole measure of our commercial
relations, the guage of all our commercial
greatness.

It has been this active, business-loving spirit
that has prevented the Australians even in the
interior from falling into those indolent and
nomadic habits which have generally charac-
terised the " keepers of sheep ;" and which,
under other circumstances, might especially
have been engendered on the wild and far-
spreading plains of this colony. It is true
some may regret that the simplicity and soft-
ness of character which is said to prevail
amongst most pastoral races have been lost in
this more energetic spirit ; but it is impossible
to doubt that, in dealing with the stern realities
of life, a greater amount of good to the community and to the world at large will be done,
and consequently a greater amount of the blessings of civilization attained.

There is one light in which we may dwell
with complacency on the preservation of this
quick, active, British spirit of enterprise, even
amidst the quiet and enervating pursuits in
which so large a share of the population has
been engaged.

It gives good hope for the future. It encourages us to believe that, as the production of wool has not degenerated us into the semicivilization of nomadic tribes, neither will the production of gold plunge us into those habits of indolent sensuality, reckless ferocity, or selfish cupidity which have so frequently accompanied the production of the precious metals in other parts of the world. It is our belief that, instead of crushing or subduing this commercial spirit, the discovery of gold will stimulate it ; it is another instrument in our hands to extend our enterprise,—it is another and a giant engine to propel the vessel of Australian commerce with increased rapidity.

It is this spirit that will rob gold of those mere selfish and sordid considerations which have made other gold-producing communities indolent and supine, and we will hope that this spirit, based on British principle and carefully nurtured by British honesty and British liberality, will preserve us from the vices and depravity which have but too often followed on the glittering but dangerous gift.

In accounting for this national characteristic, if we may so call it, of the Australian people, and particularly of the people of New South Wales, it may be remarked that, to a very considerable extent, a tone had been given to the manners and habits of the people before the pursuit of woolgrowing was engaged in to any great extent. The continual arrival of vessels with convicts and emigrants from

England rendered commercial establishments to some extent necessary. Wharves and stores sprang up, and the capabilities of the splendid harbour of Port Jackson to become the great emporium of trade in the Pacific were soon seen and appreciated. The Southern fisheries held out peculiar attractions to the bold and hardy adventurers of whom the early colonists chiefly consisted; and the splendid success which met the enterprise of those who engaged in this pursuit tended to the creation and rapid increase of the colonial marine. The gradual establishment and growth of the sister colonies,—the advantages offered by the extension of our commerce to China,—all followed in their turn; and Sydney soon assumed the aspect of a busy commercial seaport town.

We must however proceed to trace the growth and history of the commerce of New South Wales a little more minutely.

As the basis of all commerce we must in the first instance refer to the monetary systems which have at different times prevailed in the colony.

After the first settlement, for upwards of thirty years, the circulating medium of the colony consisted of the private notes of individuals. These were sometimes issued to a considerable extent by merchants and traders, who in this respect added to their ordinary business the functions of bankers. They were however issued by private individuals, shopkeepers, publicans and others, to meet the emergencies of their own business, and these notes varied in amount from hundreds of pounds down to 6d.

F'oating and insecure paper of this description was of course subject to much depreciation, and the evils of the system were felt very severely.

In the year 1817, the first Bank was established in the colony, under the title of the Bank of New South Wales. This Bank was incorporated under the seal of the colony, its capital stock being £20,000, raised in shares of £100 each. The notes issued by this Bank were for 2s. 6d., 5s., 10s.. £1, and £5. In the first year of its incorporation the bills discounted by the Bank amounted to only £12,193. In 1818, they rose to £81,672; in 1819, to £107,256. The dividend declared in 1818, was at the rate of 12 per cent.; in 1819, it was 21 per cent.; in 1820 and 21, 12 per cent.; in 1822, 15 per cent. The Bank has continued to flourish to this day, of course under many modifications and alterations of its constitution, its capital being gradually extended to £150,000.

The Bank of Australia was established in 1826, with a capital of £220,000. A small proportion only of which, however, was paid up. This bank was also a bank of issue and deposit, and for a long period of years it maintained an outward appearance of great prosperity. The high dividends paid, however, were fictitious, and a reckless system of advances to merchants and others engaged in reckless speculations involved it in the vortex of insolvency, which whirled the mercantile affairs of the colony nearly into total ruin, in the years 1843 and 1844. The insolvency of this bank involved a large number of its shareholders in the deepest distress, many of them being widows and retired officers, who had nothing else to depend on. It is however to the credit of the colony to state that after stupendous efforts the whole of the liabilities of the bank, amounting to upwards of £200,000, have been paid off.

In the year 1834, a London company, under the title of the Bank of Australasia, was established and incorporated by royal charter, with a capital of £200,000, for the purpose of establishing banks of issue in the various Australian settlements. The Sydney branch commenced business the 14th October, 1835; and branches were subsequently established at Maitland, Melbourne, Hobart Town, and Adelaide. The bank suffered severely from the failure of the Bank of Australia, to which it had advanced, on promissory notes, upwards of £160,000. It has however since recovered itself, and is now paying a dividend.

The Commercial Bank was established in 1834, and was incorporated by Act of the Legislative Council; its capital was £150,000, and it has also been a very flourishing concern.

In 1838 another London Company entitled the Union Bank of Australia was established.

This company declined to be incorporated, and is a mere partnership with an unlimited liability, and unlimited circulation. This bank has branch establishments throughout the Australasian colonies, and from the excellent management of its affairs it has been highly profitable to the shareholders.

The charters of incorporation of the New South Wales Bank and the Commercial Bank have since been remodelled by local enactments, and at present the principles on which they are based are briefly as follows :—The liability of each shareholder is limited to twice the amount of his shares. The whole amount of capital must be paid up in two years—the circulation of notes is limited to the amount of capital.

The issue and liability of the shareholders of the Bank of Australasia are regulated by the same principles as govern English Banking Companies.

The issue and liability of the Union Bank of Australia are both unlimited.

Under a local enactment, all these banks are required to furnish to the Government for publication in the *Government Gazette*, a half-yearly statement showing the amount and nature of the debts, engagements, and liabilities, and of the assets and property or securities of the respective bank; also, a quarterly general abstract, showing the average amount of the liabilities and assets of the respective bank taken from the several weekly statements during the quarter.

Such is the system of banking which has now been established in the colony, and under which the currency of the colony is governed. The notes issued by these four banks form almost entirely the circulating medium of the colony, at least with the exception of silver coin. And although, no doubt, it is not a system which would theoretically bear the strict scrutiny of financiers, it has been found practically to work beneficially. The most unlimited confidence is felt in the stability of the banks, and their notes are always passed from hand to hand without the slightest depreciation or distrust.

That this is not a mere vulgar feeling of security, arising from ignorance or apathy, it is enough to say that in the year 1850, a select committee appointed to enquire into the whole system of banking, having taken the evidence of the managers of all the banks of the colony, reported that it would not be expedient to introduce a metallic currency into the colony, or to recommend at present any alteration in the laws affecting it.

We now proceed to show the present position of the Banks. The aggregate note circulation of the Banks in the colony of New South Wales alone, in the quarter ending June 1852, was £600,400 ; of these £169,500 were issued by the Bank of New South Wales ; £125,600 by the Commercial Bank ; £119,900 by the Bank of Australasia ; £185,400, by the Union Bank.

The aggregate amount of deposits held by the four banks at the same period was £1,648,100. Of these, £686,100 were held by the Bank of New South Wales ; £308,100, by the Commercial Bank ; £314,800, by the Bank of Australasia ; £339,100, by the Union Bank.

The aggregate of coin and bullion held by the banks, was £769,100, being £354,700 in the Bank of New South Wales ; £96,300, in the Commercial Bank ; £118,700, in the Bank of Australasia ; £199,400, in the Union Bank.

The aggregate amount of the discounts of the banks was £1,390,100 ; or £430,000 by the Bank of New South Wales, £319,700 by the Commercial Bank, £289,500 by the Bank of Australasia, and £350,900 by the Union Bank.

This brief sketch of the monetary system of the colony, will be sufficient to indicate the extent of those commercial transactions which can only be represented and effected by the means of the financial operations which the banks are instituted to facilitate.

We now come to consider the trade of the colony, and for this purpose it is unnecessary that we should turn back farther than the year 1830.

In the year 1830, the total population of the colony, as near as it could be arrived at at that day, was about 55,000. The amount of the imports into the colony in that year was £420,480 ; arriving in 157 vessels, of a tonnage of 31,225. The amount of exports was £141,461, exported in 149 vessels, of a tonnage of 28,822.

In 1840, the imports into the colony amounted to £2,600,650, or an increase of eleven fold in ten years. In the same year the exports amounted to £1,270,823, or an increase of nine fold in ten years.

In the year 1850, the imports were £1,333,413, being a decrease in the ten years from 1840, of 100 per cent. In the same year the exports were £1,357,784, being an increase over 1843 of about ten per cent.

It is, however, necessary to state that in the year 1840 the trade of the colony was inflated beyond all precedent. The supposed inexhaustible wealth of our pastures and the high prices paid for our wool in England, induced speculation to an enormous extent. The unlimited credit which prevailed in the colony stimulated the spirit here, while the hope of enormous profits induced the English merchants to increase consignments to an extravagant degree. The consequences of this rash inflation of the ordinary business of the colony were ruinous; it was the precursor of the insolvency which followed three years after, fatal both to the speculations of the Australian colonist and the hopes of the British merchant, three-fourths of the importations of 1840 being sold under the hammer below prime cost in succeeding years.

In 1851 the total amount of imports into the colony was £1,563,931, consisting of £1,152,421 from Great Britain, £15,609 from New Zealand, £174,250 from other colonies, £6771 from the South Sea Islands, £23,033 from the Fisheries, £14,127 from the United States of America, and £177,720 from foreign states.

The exports of the year 1851 amounted to £1,796,912, being £1,477,452 to Great Britain; £94,046 to New Zealand, £146,805 to other colonies; £15,334 to the South Sea Islands; £33,784 to the United States of America; and £29,491 to foreign states.

The imports in 1851 comprised £72,341 for wearing apparel; £10,000 for gunpowder; £25,000 for wool bags and sacks; £57,000 for beer and ale; £10,000 for blankets; £12,000 for canvas; £10,000 for coffee; £12,0000 for confections and preserves; £11,000 for cordage; £176,000 for cottons; £14,000 for drugs and medicines; £18,000 for earthenware and china; £32,500 for flour and bread; £10,000 for fruits; £11,000 for glass; £32,000 for grain (including rice); £84,000 for haberdashery; £68,000 for hardware; £11,000 for hats and bonnets; £7000 for hosiery and gloves; £6000 for slops; £14,000 for iron and steel; £19000 for leather boots and shoes; £92,000 for linens; £10,000 for nails; £35,000 for oils; £44,000 for oilmen's stores; £13,000 for silks; £60,000 for spirits; £41,000 for stationary, books, and papers; £108,608 for sugar; £48,000 for tea; £54,000 for tobacco and cigars; £33,000 for wine; £151,000 for woollens and a very long list of other articles imported in smaller quantities.

The exports of 1851, comprised wool, £828,342; tallow, £114,168; horses, £17,298; other live stock, £6,000; oil, £26,000; salted and preserved meats, £9,000; horned cattle, £22,600; coals, £12,000. These were all the produce of the colony; the rest of the exports comprise chiefly British and foreign goods sent to the surrounding colonies.

The total population of the colony on the 31st December, 1851, was 197,168, so that the amount of imports to every man, woman, and child in the colony, would be at the rate of about £8 a-head, and of exports about £9 a-head, a rate which we believe is hardly equalled by any community in the world.

The import trade of New South Wales comprises several branches of greater or less importance.

The principal of these imports are from the mother country, comprising nearly £1,200,000 of the principal articles of manufacture of that country. Next in importance is the trade from Manila and the China Seas, consisting chiefly of tea, sugar, and cigars, amounting to nearly £200,000 per annum. An examination of the trade with Manila, proves very clearly the importance of these colonies to that settlement, in a commercial point of view. The rapid growth for the last few years, and the present importance of the trade between Manila and the Australasian colonies, is not generally known and appreciated. In the year 1849 the exportation of sugar from Manila to these colonies was 86,546 piculs, or just one-half what was imported into Great Britain. In 1850, the export increased to 135,819 piculs, and in 1851 to 180,988 piculs, or just 20,000 piculs more than was exported to Great Britain and the whole continent of Europe, and 50,000 piculs more than was exported to the United States. In 1849 the export of cigars to these colonies was 7277 M.; in 1850, 10,938 M.; in 1851, 16,270 M.; while in the latter year the export to Great Britain was 7295 M.; to the United States, 2532 M.; to the Continent of Europe, 4981 M., or 14,778 M. in all being 1492 M. less than the export to these colonies. The total export of sugar from Manila in 1851, was 508,835 piculs, of which we took nearly two-fifths; the total export of cigars 66,207 M., of which we took one-fourth; the total export of coffee, 15,267 piculs, of which we took one-fifth.

With regard to this trade it must be borne in mind, that these exports are paid for in cash only—as there is very little export trade to Manila, or any other port in the China Seas.

The next most important branch of this trade is the inter-colonial trade. This is very important as regards our commercial position. From the neighbouring colonies of Van Dieman's Land and South Australia and New Zealand, we obtain principally produce—

breadstuffs, potatoes, fruits, and metallic ores.

In return for these New South Wales is to no inconsiderable extent the medium through which these colonies receive their supplies of British and foreign goods. At all events in the absence of sufficient supplies direct, Sydney is resorted to as the market, and it is very necessary for the mercantile interests to encourage the growth of these feelings, and be prepared to meet the demand, as it is only by doing this that Sydney can maintain its position as the emporium of the trade of the Southern Seas.

The trade from the South Sea Islands is also important in a mercantile point of view. Although in 1851 it amounted only to £6,771 in the previous year it was £31,827. The articles imported are cocoanut oil, sandal wood, &c., which form articles of export to foreign countries and serve to stimulate the spirit of commercial enterprise.

There is every probability that in the course of a few years a large and valuable trade may spring up with these islands, the fertility and capabilities of which as well as the general intelligence of their inhabitants, are far more appreciated now than they were a few years ago.

Another branch of trade is an uncertain one, being the trade in bread stuffs, from the west coast of South America in seasons of scarcity. There is no export trade to balance these occasional importations, which are consequently paid for in money.

The trade from foreign states, (except those which we have specially referred to,) is very small. An occasional cargo of wine from Spain or Portugal,—a miscellaneous cargo from the United States, once, or perhaps twice a year, and of late such little cargos as a few German emigrant ships may bring with them,—comprise the whole; but it is not too much to expect that under the influence of the repeal of the Navigation laws, the gold discovery, and above all, the abolition of all Customs' restrictions on foreign produce, native or manu_factured, that the commercial intercourse of the colony of New South Wales with foreign states, will very soon be very largely increased.

The export trade is more simple, out of an amount of £1,796 9s. 10d.—£1,477,452 being sent home to the mother country—the exports to the neighbouring colonies amount to £240,000; to the South Sea Islands £15,334; and to the United States of America, £95,473; most part of this latter amount being accounted for by the trade lately sprung up between Sydney and California. The exports to foreign states was in 1851, £29,491, being 120 per cent. increase in this class of exports on the previous year, shewing that the alteration in the Navigation laws had already begun to have its effect. There has also been for some years past a trade in horses to India; this amounted in 185 , to £17,298.

D 4

The statistics of the shipping of the colony also afford evidence of the steady growth of its commerce.

In the year 1841, the number of vessels entered inwards was 442, of a tonnage of 131,278; in the year 1851, the number of vessels was 553, tonnage 153,002.

In the latter year these vessels comprised from Great Britain 73, tonnage 40,867; from other colonies 271, tonnage 57,766; from the South Sea Islands 40, tonnage 5,643; from the Fisheries 33, tonnage 8,430; from the United States of America (including California) 72, tonnage, 20,473; from other Foreign States 64, tonnage 19,822.

In 1841, the shipping entered outwards was, vessels 462, tonnage 137,962; in 1851, it was vessels 503, tonnage 139,020, comprising to Great Britain 54, tonnage 26,694; to other colonies 278, tonnage 55,741; to the South Sea Islands 32, tonnage 5,513; to the Fisheries 33, tonnage 9,658; to the United States of America (including California) 26, tonnage 9,457; to Foreign States, 80, tonnage 31,957.

We now turn our attention to the system of commercial government, under which the commerce of the colony has hitherto been carried on.

With regard to export duties, the small duty formerly charged on colonial wool admitted into the mother country was abolished a few years ago, and almost every other description of colonial produce is admitted duty free.

The import duties, with the exception of spirits and tobacco, were, until the present year, an ad valorem duty of 15 per cent. on all articles of foreign produce or foreign manufacture. British goods were admitted free. The duty on foreign tobacco was 2s. per lb. ; and on brandy and gin 6s. per gallon ; rum and whiskey, 3s. 6d. per gallon.

During the session of the Legislative Council of 1852 however, a new tariff has been established, based on free trade principles, and the duties now charged on goods imported to New South are solely as follows:—Ale and beer, in wood 1d. per gallon ; ale and beer in bottle, 3d. per gallon ; coffee, chocolate, and cocoa, ¾d. per lb. ; currants, raisins, and other dried fruits, ½d. per lb. ; brandy, proof strength, 6s. per gallon ; gin, ditto, 6s. per gallon ; rum, and all other spirits, 4s. per gallon ; perfumed spirits, of whatever strength, 4s. per gallon ; all spirits, liqueurs, cordials, brandied fruits, or strong waters, 6s. per gallon ; refined sugar, 3s. 4d. per cwt. ; unrefined ditto, 2s. 6d. per cwt. ; molasses, 1s. 8d. per cwt. ; tea, 1½d. per. lb. ; manufactured tobacco, other than cigars and snuffs, 1s. 6d., until the 31st day of December, 1853, and thereafter, 1s. ; unmanufactured tobacco, 1s. per lb. until 31st December, 1843, and thereafter 8d. per lb. ; cigars and snuffs, 2s. per lb. ; wine, 1s. per gallon.

The eminent simplicity of this tariff has

created the highest satisfaction throughout the colony. The duties on spirits and tobacco being articles of luxury, and the use of which indeed a wise policy would as far as prudent resist, can be no burden on any one.

The duty on tea and sugar is one which will operate so equally and will so universally effect all classes, that no injustice can be inflicted by it ; and if it cause a fractional advance in the price of these articles to the consumer, the absence of taxation on all other articles will enable him to procure those articles at a proportionably cheaper rate. As long as a revenue must be raised by taxation for revenue purposes the one great principle to be observed is to make that taxation bear equally on all, and it is wise therefore to confine duties to those articles only which are of very general consumption.

It is confidently anticipated that this altera- tion of the Tariff will have a most beneficial effect, both as regards the amount of revenue collected, and the encouragement it will give to trade. Concurrently with the passing of this Act, all port and harbour dues, and all auction duties, were repealed, and it may perhaps be said, that New South Wales affords the first example of a great commercial community, abandoning almost without exception the legis- lative restrictions by which trade has been hitherto governed.

The wisdom of this course it is not the object of these papers either to prove or disprove ; and yet we may venture to indulge in the hope that it was a prudent and a happy course for a young nation starting in full vigour into the commerce of the world, to lay aside those restrictions and limitations, which the experience of older and more matured nations have found too cumbersome to be borne. Free and unfettered to carry her produce to any of the countries of the world, to go in the pride of her wealth—in gold, in wool, in wine, and in oil, to all the markets of the habitable globe to purchase for herself the things she needeth; what prescience of wisdom — what spirit of prophecy shall discern and unfold the commercial eminence to which this great colony may aspire. On the extreme verge of the south eastern Pacific a few years perhaps will see a mighty city—a majestic empire—rolling back to the northern and western world the treasures of her soil the produce of her vineyards and her fields, the fabrics of her looms, and of her factories, the glories of her art, and the wonders of her science, to prove that the seed scattered on the footsteps of civilization, trampling on the elements, and annihilating space has not been sown in vain.

It would scarcely be expected that we should conclude this branch of our subject without some enquiry into the changes which the recent discovery of gold will have upon the commerce of this country.

That it will exercise a vast influence must be apparent to all, but whether that influence will be for good or ill is a disputed question. It is however difficult to suppose that in a country where the value of wealth and the active use of it for the purposes of increase are so well understood, this wonderful addition to the natural resources should not be productive of increased prosperity.

It is true that at present the production of very large quantities of gold has been productive of considerable monetary confusion. The enormous increase in the amount of exports thus caused has turned the balance of trade so strongly in favour of this country that the exchanges have undergone alterations extremely adverse to our interests. The excess of exports over imports renders the amount of the balance due from Great Britain to this country large, and consequently the amount of bills drawn on London against that excess of exports is large, while the demand for such bills is small.

The ordinary rule which governs supply and demand has consequently had its natural effect, and bills on England have fallen to a low discount—bank bills to eight per cent and private bills to 12 per cent. If this consequence had affected operations in gold alone it would have been a matter of comparatively little consequence, but operating as it must on all descriptions of produce it has proved seriously detrimental to those industrial pursuits which were already languishing from the abstraction from them of the

labour which has been attracted to the gold
fields.   That the evil, loss, and confusion thus
caused has been great, it is impossible to doubt,
but a vast increase to the weath of a nation, by
the sudden development of its latent resources
has seldom proved an unmixed good.

The evil however is not likely to be of long
continuance, and the remedy for it, is likely,
although it may not repair individual losses, to
compensate   the   colony   most   amply   for   its
temporary distresses.

It has been proposed by the Legislative
Council of the colony, and has been assented
to by the British Government, that a branch of
the royal mint shall be established in Sydney.

This, with the exception of the Indian dependencies, is the first instance of the establishment of a mint in a British colony, for the
simple reason that in no other dependency of
the Crown have the precious metals been produced in sufficient quantities to warrant such
an establishment.

The mint in Sydney will be restricted to a
gold coinage, identical in all respects to that
of   England,   and   subjected   to   periodical
tests by the officers of the mint in England.
Of course any distinctive mark between the
colonial and the imperial coin would at once
tend to the depreciation of the former.

What effect the establishment of a mint in
the colony, where gold is so plentiful, may
have upon the currency of the colony it is
difficult to say, but it does not seem very

probable, even though sovereigns should be abundant, that they will supplant the issues of the banks as a circulating medium.

It is, however, likely that fixing a certain arbitrary price to gold of a certain standard, or giving the possessor of such gold the power to turn it into coin at will, will lead to an alteration in the basis of the bank issues, and that the colonial banks will hereafter limit their issues in proportion to the amount of coin or bullion they have in their possession, as in England, instead of their being limited, as at present, by the amount of their paid up capital.

For use in the colony, then it is improbable that the coinage will be extensive ; and for the purpose of shipment or remittance, the exact value having been ascertained, gold in bullion would be more convenient, and to the extent of the cost of coinage, cheaper.

There may, however, be a considerable coinage for the purpose of paying for those importations, for which the colony has to pay in money, and the settlement of these accounts will probably be made in sovereigns, instead of bills on Europe.

But the most beneficial effect which the mint must have, will be to restore the equilibrium of the Exchanges, for when gold becomes convertible into coin on the spot, at a fixed rate, all demands for advances against shipments of the precious metal to England will cease. As far as the Exchange goes, therefore gold, will cease to operate, and leave it to those trifling variations which are regulated by the excess or the deficiency in the ordinary exports of the country.

Left to assert their own importance, there need be little fear that these industrial pursuits will dwindle and decay. The imminent danger which now threatens them, will prove their most effective and permanent defence.

Without the gold fields, the ordinary supply of labour (while to procure it would have deprived the colony of the means of perfecting those means of internal communication, almost as necessary as labour itself) would have been miserably stinted. Now however no calculation can place the limit to voluntary Immigration, while common sense tells us that the numbers that can be profitably engaged or that can be subsisted at the gold diggings, will soon find their maximum.

Any increase of population in excess of this maximum must resort to the ordinary occupations of labour, and thus a permanent and extended industrial class will be created.

We repeat our conviction that the enterprising spirit of the colony will not be subdued by the enervating influences of gold. Gold will be valued not as wealth, not as capital, but as the creator of wealth and capital. It will be sought here to give value to the baser metals, by turning them to useful apppliances. It will be sought for to bring together in frequent communication the remote ends of this vast continent. It will be sought for to

people the wilderness and to reclaim the
desert; to nerve and invigorate the sinews of
this youthful commercial nation till they
harden into the giant-strength of its glorious
maturity.

MANUFACTURES.

In the course of previous papers, we have had
frequent occasion to notice the great natural
resources which New South Wales possessess
for the manufacture of useful and valuable
articles of commerce.

In the present paper, we shall bring more
closely together those facts which bear most
strongly on this branch of trade, and show as
far as the means we possess admit, the progress
which has been made in manufacturing arts in
the colony.

If the developement of these resources and
their application should appear to be slow, it
must be remembered that the same excuse
holds good for manufactures as for every other
pursuit except wool growing; that there has
been little or no labour to spare to devote to them.

To create a manufacturing trade, would
engross and concentrate a large amount of
labour, more severe in its character, and at
first at least, more slow in its returns than
agricultural and pastoral pursuits; while the
skill and experience essential for the first may
be to a considerable extent dispensed with in
the last.

Of course from the earliest settlement, some rude manufactures have existed, such as of simple articles of necessity, and the ruder implements required in other pursuits.

But it has been naturally the bent of the policy which has directed the energies of this country, to make its production of staple materials of manufactures the first object, rather than to turn them to account on the spot. Because by exporting them to Great Britain, they were there manufactured at less expense, to the great benefit of the manufacturing interests at home, and at the same time the wealth they gave to the colonists, rendered Australia a most valuable market for a large share of these manufactures.

Although it is desirable now to a considerable extent, that manufactures should be gradually encouraged, there is no reason to regret that this almost exclusive export of material and almost exclusive import of manufactures should have prevailed. To have circumscribed the limit of our wants by providing for them all ourselves, would have been to have cramped and confined our energies, and to have dulled the spirit of enterprise which prevails so strongly amongst us.

We should never become a great manufacturing country if this were the case, and it is much wiser that manufacturing enterprise, as far as mere home consumption goes, should be restrained until, added to our own wants, we are enabled to supply those of surrounding and even distant communities. As it was by growing wool for export we became a great sheep farming country, without degenerating into a mere pastoral community, so it will be by encouraging manufactures as another great ingredient in the commercial enterprise of the colony, that we shall be enabled to take our stand in these seas as the rival of European and American artificers.

The manufactures of the colony are at present very limited, and they have in fact, in some branches, considerably diminished of late years.

Three years after the foundation of the colony brickmaking commenced, and the first brick building built of colonial made bricks was erected in 1791. In 1805, the first sailing vessel was built; in 1815, the first steam-engine was worked in the colony. In 1820, colonial tobacco was first manufactured, and colonial spirits first distilled; and in 1831, the first colonial steam-boat was launched.

There were two distilleries established in the year 1837, and these have remained in full work, except at short intervals, up to the present time. Under the old system of very high duties on foreign spirits, these distilleries made large profits, but even these were insufficient to satisfy the proprietors, and illicit distillation took place to a considerable extent in

1846 ; however more stringent regulations for the inspection of distilleries were enacted, and the duty on foreign rum was reduced from 7s. 6d. to 3s. 6d. The profits of the distillers then began to fall off, and the largest of them was compelled to shut up, but it has recently been again set at work by a sugar refining company, and the two distilleries are now turning out from 7000 to 10,000 gallons weekly. Nearly the whole of the spirits distilled in this colony, are manufactured from sugar and molasses.

In addition to these distilleries, there is one extensive rectifying and compounding establishment, and in former years there were three or four. In the year 1837, there were 7 breweries,—three in Sydney ; two in Parramatta ; one in Windsor ; and one in Maitland. In 1844 there were 12 ; in 1845 there were 15 ; in 1846, 16 ; in 1847, 15 ; in 1848, 12 ; in 1849, 21 ; in 1850, 19 ; in 1851, 17.

The beer brewed at these breweries is drank to a very considerable extent in the colony by the humbler classes, but a very large portion of it is an unwholesome beverage, being adulterated with many deleterious articles. Medical men have attributed death in many instances to the excessive use of this drink. The two largest breweries in the colony are in Sydney, and as they are carried on by men of respectability and large capital, the profits are large.

The quantity of beer consumed in the colony is very large, as in addition to the home-made the importation of the article in 1851 amounted to £57,000.

The colonial beer is very inferior to the British, and is sold at less than half the price. It is probable however that a better article will soon be produced to supply the deficiency of English beer which frequently exists. One of the Sydney brewers has lately succeeded in producing a beer which successfully competed with the English beverage for some months.

There are two sugar refining companies in the colony, one of which has been established ten years the other four.

The Australasian Sugar Refining Company carries on a very large trade, supplying not only nearly the whole of the home consumption but also the wants of the neighbouring colonies. The raw sugar is procured for the most part from Manila, and the trade to that settlement is much encouraged by these establishments. The prices charged by the company for its sugar in ordinary times are about 45s. per cwt. for loaf, and 34s. per cwt. for crystallized.

The quantity of refined sugar manufactured in 1847 was, 39,600 cwt.; in 1848, 26,000 cwt.; in 1849, 35,000 cwt.; in 1850, 51,000 cwt.; in 1851, 74,000 cwt.

There are twelve soap and candle manufacturers in the colony, and they produce a considerable quantity of both articles both

for home consumption and for exportation.

With the exception of sperm candles, indeed,
the whole colony is supplied by the home
manufactories.

The colonial soap has of late years nearly
superseded the English article, which used to
be imported in large quantities. The soap
made in the colony is preferred for use, while it
is produced at a cost of about 3d. per lb. The
quantity of soap manufactured in 1847 was
19,925 cwt.; in 1848, 18,900 cwt.; in 1849,
24,623 cwt.; in 1850, 25,986 cwt.; in 1851,
33,065 cwt.

There are at present only six manufactories
of tobacco in the colony, but in 1849, there
were fifteen; and in 1850, fourteen. These,
however, were on a small scale, and the quantity manufactured was but small.

Many samples of tobacco grown and manufactured in the colony have been pronounced
by competent judges equal to Virginian; but
a very considerable prejudice exists against it.
There is, however, no doubt, that the dealers
dispose of a great deal as American tobacco
and get a high price for it. The reduction of
the duties on foreign tobacco in the last session
of the Council will probably retard the progress of the production and manufacture of
this article; but with an abundance of labor,
there is no question that this branch of
industry will be again profitably resorted to.
The quantity of tobacco manufactured in 1847,

was 1321 cwt.; in 1848, 714 cwt.; in 1849, 2758 cwt.; in 1850, 3833 cwt.; in 1851, 4841 cwt.

There are five woollen cloth manufactories in the colony, the largest of which is the Messrs. Byrnes', at Parramatta. This establishment is very extensive, and is conducted by its enterprising proprietors on the true British principle. There was also a large manufactory at Stockton, but the works have been interfered with by a serious fire, which took place there some time back, and this accounts for the falling off in the production last year. The cloths principally manufactured in the colony are tweeds, and the quality of these has been much improved in the last few years.

The quantity of cloth and tweeds manufactured in the colony in 1847, was 175,088 yards; in 1848, 164,749 yards; in 1849, 180,197 yards; in 1850, 190,791 yards; in 1851, 114,394 yards.

In addition to these larger factories there are two hat manufactories, fifty-five tanneries, nine salting and meat preserving establishments, four potteries, two copper smelting establishments, and fifteen iron and brass foundries.

The export of unmanufactured leather is very considerable, amounting in 1851 to 562 215 lbs., valued at £11,665. The consumption of colonial leather in the colony is also very large, both for shoes and boots, and for coach building and harness.

The other establishments we have enumerated, are chiefly employed in supplying the colonial consumption.

The lighter handicrafts in a small way are pursued with great avidity and considerable skill in the towns of the colony, especially in Sydney. There are plenty of expert jewellers; and the articles of colonial workmanship, manufactured from colonial gold and colonial gems, would, in many instances, do credit to London establishments. Furniture, and some of the larger articles of cabinetware, are also manufactured with much taste in the colony. Many of the woods of the colony are peculiarly appropriate to this trade, which, we have no doubt, will one day assume a very considerable importance. There are also one or two small cutlery establishments; but though very good knives and scissors, and even surgical instruments have been made in the colony, the colonial workmen are principally employed in repairing such instruments.

As might be expected in a colony so much and so actively engaged in mercantile pursuits, ship-building has been engaged in to a very considerable extent, and the colonial vessels for the most part, both as models, and as to their soundness, and durability, are highly creditable to the country. Fortunately there is an abundance of excellent timber suited for every department of ship-building, and it is highly important that this useful art should be carefully encouraged.

In 1840, the vessels built in the colony were 17; tonnage, 1196. In 1841, 33; tonnage, 2037. In 1842, 25; tonnage, 1297. In 1843,

41; tonnage, 1231. In 1844, 15; tonnage, 498. In 1845, 15; tonnage, 931. In 1846, 27; tonnage 1013. In 1847, 33; tonnage, 2122. In 1848, 26; tonnage, 1281. In 1849, 35; tonnage, 1720. In 1850, 36; tonnage, 1605. In 1851, 24; tonnage, 939.

Although therefore, New South Wales cannot assume the character of a manufacturing country, yet these pursuits are sufficiently engaged in to excite the desire of turning her resources for such pursuits to the best account.

These resources are equalled by few countries in the world, either in extent or variety. Her flocks and herds afford the materials for the manufacture of woollens and leather, and her mineral treasures offer inexhaustible materials for almost every branch of British trade. Glass, at the lowest prices, and of the finest quality, can be made from the sand that abounds in almost every district of the colony; while earthenware and porcelain of the finest and most homely descriptions are provided for in the clays and the detritus of the granite formations, which so largely prevail. The annual destruction in the colony of the materials for the manufacture of paper is seldom thought of, and yet it must be immense, while the consumption of the article is proportionably extensive. In addition to the demand for the ordinary purposes of trade, there are four large daily newspapers in this colony and Victoria, with an average circulation equal to that of almost any English paper, except the *Times*.

Hemp and flax can be cultivated profitably to an illimitable extent, and thus the materials for the manufacture of linens are within our reach. While the semi-tropical districts in the North must sooner or later be covered with cotton plantations, which will enable us in this hemisphere to vie with the factories of Lancashire.

True, even after the first shock of the gold discovery shall be got over, labour and capital, —extensively as they will have been introduced, — will be devoted principally to the production and export of staple articles. But each succeeding year will augment the wealth derived from this production, till it must seek another investment. Each succeeding year will enlarge the class of population, who either cannot find room in the pursuits of pasture and agriculture or who turn with distaste from those pursuits. This surplus capital, this surplus labour, will naturally cling to a domestic investment and employment, rather than turn to foreign countries to seek either, and will seize with avidity the advantages offered to manufacturing enterprise in the colony.

The more selfish spirit, spirit, the short-sightedness of which no experience can altogether repress, and the abstract principle of which is perhaps to some extent correct—the spirit of self-dependence ; the desire to provide for all our own wants with our own hands,

will be at work.   But once make that spirit
active —once give life and vigour to enterprise
in this direction, and the bounds of home
supply will soon be reached ; the limits of
home consumption will soon be overstepped.

The whole domain of the Southern Pacific
will become the field which must be supplied
from our pastures, our vineyards, our cotton
plantations, and manufactories.

The surrounding colonies, and the settlements of Eastern Asia, will first occupy our
attention and our enterprise ; but these too in
their turn will prove too confined to give our
energies full scope ; and at last we, like our
fathers before us, shall join in the work of
civilization, and provide markets for ourselves
by the colonization of the innumerable islands
which stud the expanse that divides us from
the older world.

PART VII.

Present state and future prospects of the Colony.

The object of the series of papers, of which this forms the concluding number, was to afford simple information as to the capabilities of the colony of New South Wales for the maintenance of civilized man ; and of the nature and variety of those occupations of industry which were open to, and would repay the labour and skill devoted to them.

They were written in especial regard to the instruction of intending or newly-arrived immigrants, and it was believed that, in a collected form, they would form a useful hand-book to direct and guide the inexperienced colonist in the choice of a vocation, and probably afford him some useful and profitable hints in following out that vocation. Since, however, these papers were commenced, the change which has passed over these colonies has been so vast, that in order to make the work really useful it was thought advisable to defer its completion until the future prospects of the colony, under the influence of the gold discovery, had assumed some palpable distinctness, by which the statements of the previous papers might be measured and weighed.

It is with considerable satisfaction that the writers find, that, although the relation as to the importance of various pursuits has altered, they have little to correct and nothing to recal in their descriptions of the products, manufactures, and commerce of the colony, or as to the profit which each of these great branches of progressive civilization will yield.

The object, then, of this article will be simply to explain the altered circumstances of the colony, its extraordinary advance in wealth and prosperity since the commencement of these papers, and its consequent fitness or unfitness for those branches of industry, the details of which have been more minutely examined in previous papers.

To this it may be well to add such reflections on the future prospects of the colony as the present aspect of things appears to warrant.

It is necessary in the first instance that a few statistics should be afforded in order that the progression of the colony may be fully understood.

The only authoritative official statistics published in this colony are the returns furnished annually by the Government, and these unfortunately extend only to the termination of the year 1851, but as it was in that year these papers were commenced the data they afford will be sufficient for our purpose.

In that year the total population of the colony amounted to 190,000.

In 1853, this number, by natural increase

and by immigration, was probably increased by some 20,000 people, whilst the immigration alone for the first quarter of the present year, amounts to upwards of 8000.

On the score of increased population, then every branch of industrial production must have become more essentially desirable, whether that production be for consumption, as for instance, in the pursuit of agriculture, or for exportation and sale with the view to purchase foreign commodities, as in pastoral pursuits and gold digging.

And it is to be observed that in a new country like New South Wales, where extreme prosperity and consequent extreme individual wealth prevails, the accumulating amount of labour is by no means equal to the accumulating amount of consumption. Consequently up to a limit which it would be idle for us to calculate here, industrial pursuits will, under a healthy state of things, increase in the profit they afford in proportion to the increase of population. This is in accordance with the natural rule of supply and demand, because in this country the individual consumption and individual acquisition of wealth is greater than the individual amount of labour introduced at the ordinary price of such labour, and consequently the demand for such labour is greater than the supply

The reverse of this obtains generally in old and thickly peopled countries, where the maximum of population, and therefore of labour, rules, and the very lowest rate of consumption prevails.

We find then in the rapid increase of the population of the colony, and the probable maintenance even in a larger ratio of a progressive increase, the surest guarantee that the development of all the industrial resources we have described will be advantageous and profitable, while we have equal assurance from the varied wants of a wealthy community like this, that no one of these resources can be left stagnant, without damage to the interests, the comforts, or the luxuries of the community.

To explain the position we have assumed, it is only necessary to illustrate it by a few facts.

In regard to the production of articles of consumption in this colony, these are mainly referable to the pursuit of agriculture in some shape or other. Now, taking the article of grain—we believe the production in 1852 will be found to be equal to that of 1851, but the importation of breadstuffs during the former year will exceed that of the latter five-fold, although the increase of population has only been in the ratio of about one-fifth.

We will now proceed to examine another test of the progression of the colony during the last year. In 1851, the amount of imports into the colony from all countries, was £1,564,000. The amount of customs duties paid on these imports was about in round numbers £190,000; we give the fullest possible amount. What the amount of imports in 1851,

was, in the absence of official returns we have no
opportunity of accurately stating. But we find
the duties paid under a reduced tariff in the
first quarter of 1853, amount to £85,000, or at
the rate of £340,000 per annum ; which according even to the calculations of 1851 would
represent an amount of imports exceeding
£2,630,000, or nearly double the total amount
of imports in the year 1851. But even this is
not a fair criterion to judge by, for by reference
to the chapter on commerce in these papers it
will be found by examination of the new
tariff that while by exemption from duty it is
probable that a large amount of merchandise
has been imported which we did not receive
in former years, the duties being levied solely
on articles of necessary consumption, the importation of duty-paying articles cannot have
decreased.

As a matter of fact it is well known that
both in 1852 and 1853, this latter class of importations has largely increased.

In the year 1851, the total amount of exports was £1,800,000. Again, from the want of
the official returns, we have no means of
accurately quoting the aggregate amount of
exports for 1852, or the first quarter of 1853, and
as we have no export duties we have no guide
to a fair calculation. But it may be stated
that it was about June 1851 that our gold
mines began to be productive, and that the
quantity shipped to the 1st January, 1852, was
only £467,000, leaving the ordinary exports of

the colony at about £1,800,000. In 1852 the gold export alone was, £2,650,000, being nearly double the total export of the preceding year, while in the first quarter of the present year it has been £910,000, or nearly at the rate of £4,000,000 per annum. It is not improbable that the export of wool and tallow during the two latter periods may have somewhat diminished, owing to the abstraction of labour from pastoral pursuits for the purpose of gold digging, but the diminution, if it be found to exist, will be so small as to deserve no weight in these calculations. In fact inasmuch as there can be no diminution in this class of exportation without some detriment to the colony, it will serve only to show that additional industry can now be more profitably employed on the pursuits from which this production arises.

As then the increase of population justly affords encouragement to the producer of articles of consumption—such as the farmer, the wine grower, and the grazier, so this vast increase in the commerce of the colony cannot fail to enlarge the profits and stimulate the enterprise of the merchant, the shopkeeper, the manufacturer, and all classes engaged in trading pursuits.

To the cultivation and acquirement then of all the various products which have been described in these papers, to the prosecution of all those schemes of industrial enterprise, the advantages of which it has been our endeavour to point out ; the discovery of gold with its increase of the wealth, commerce, and population of the colony, ought only to lend additional vigour and additional confidence.

Before entering into a more general comment on the present position of the colony, it is perhaps but right for the information of those who have no local facilities of acquiring such knowledge, to offer a few general statistics, and some passing observations in reference to subjects which it has not come strictly under these papers to touch upon.

And first in respect to education. In the year 1851 there were 423 schools in the colony, with a total of 21,120 scholars. Of this number 345 scholars we orphans, maintained and taught in Government schools ; 4,998 belonging to Church of England schools ; 891 to Wesleyan schools ; 3,310 to Roman Catholic schools; 2,861 to the National Schools ; and 6,721 to private schools.

The systems of education to which the Government affords assistance are two-fold. The Denominational System, as it is called, is carried on under the superintendence of the clergy of the respective denominations who distribute the funds furnished by the Government according to their own discretion, subject however of late years to the supervision and inspection of a board appointed by the government.

About eight years ago, the National System, or more correctly, what is known as Lord Stanley's Irish National System of Schools, was introduced. In these schools pupils of all denominations are indiscriminately received, and except in such general points of morals and belief as are universally agreed upon, Scriptural teaching is excluded; facilities are however afforded in the schools for religious instruction to the children of their respective sects by their own clergy; but as the clergy have hitherto very generally set their faces against this system, these facilities have not been taken much advantage of. The system has, however, decidedly worked well, and has progressed rapidly in popular favour; and although the excitement of the gold discovery and the migratory habits engendered by it, have disturbed its progress, still it is steadily advancing, and planting its schools throughout the scattered and remote districts of the colony, where its advantages will certainly be best appreciated and are most required.

For all this it must be confessed that educational institutions in the colony are at a very low ebb, but there seems to be a growing spirit abroad which will not rest till this important matter be remedied.

It is painful to call back reminiscences of the past of New South Wales; but the truth is ofttimes wholesome though unpalatable, and admitting as we gladly do that the emancipated proportion of the population is at present very small, yet the grown up descendants of that once numerous class, to a considerable extent, have inherited the lax morality of their parents, and the children of these, if educational institutions be not provided for them, will be reared in ignorance if not in vice. To avert this "curse of the fathers upon the children"-surely ought to be the first object of a wise and paternal government; and it is most gratifying to find that the present administration of the Government of New South Wales, has liberally and considerately lent its most favourable countenance to the promotion of education in every shape and way.

Foremost amongst these educational progressions may be ranked the establishment of the Sydney University, an institution founded on the ripest spirit of liberality, and endowed with a glorious and wise munificence. To raise the standard of education in any community there must be lofty summits for the student and the scholar to attain, from which he may look down on all below, satisfied in so far as the machinery of human instruction and learning is concerned with the eminence he has attained. Such a goal to the emulation of the youth of New South Wales, will, we believe, be furnished in the University of Sydney, when in its growth, formation, and expansion, its relief from some errors, and its freedom from many prejudices and misapprehensions, it shall in its full scope and energy serve the great and noble ends for which it was established.

This institution, although from some necessary delay in the preliminary arrangements, it has only been about eight months in practical operation, has already worked much of good to the community. A larger and more thoughtful spirit as to encouraging education of a higher order than has hitherto been afforded in the colony has been inspired ; the suggestion of the eminent professors who have been induced to emigrate to establish the University, will guide and instruct this spirit ; and with the increased appreciation of the moral, social, and physical blessings which education affords, and which is the distinguishing characteristic of the present age, combined with the abundant means which almost every class in the community possesses of paying amply for the instruction of their children, will, it may fairly be hoped and anticipated, lead shortly to as full and goodly an expansion of intellectual growth in the colony, as there has been of rapid and prosperous material progression.

In natural conjunction with the subject of educational establishments, arises the consideration of the literary institutions of the colony. Of these, again, we regret to say, we can speak in no words of high acclaim. They are few in number, and miserably inadequate to the requirements of a large, wealthy, and increasing population, with mental energies perpetually stimulated in the pursuit of material wealth.

Without the softening and ameliorating influences of literature, such a community must grow shrewd without discretion, cunning without wisdom, sordid without economy.

But the absence of literary or scientific institutions, of any note, is rather attributable to the meagerness of the means of education in the colony, than from any undervalue of literary attainment or of literary pleasure. The Government, though in some instances it has assisted literary institutions and contributed to the maintenance of some scientific ones, has displayed a somewhat niggard and paltry shortsighted economy in this respect.

We say this not so much in reference to the present day as the past, for now the colony is or ought to be capable of maintaining these institutions without aid from the Government, and both literature and science thrive more healthily in the vigorous soil of public apprebation, than in the enervating hot-bed of official patronage.

Perhaps in the long run it will be of little disadvantage to the colony that such institutions as did exist and did linger and languish under this official patronage, have nearly worn themselves out, and that the people of New South Wales have now the opportunity, with a juster apprehension of the great principles and interests involved, to found such societies as may be most suited to their wants and wishes, and best adapted for the exercise and strengthening the natural intellect of the colony.

There is but one library in the colony deserv-

ing of the name, and that, though of late
subjected to some relaxation in the rigidity of
its regulations, was in past years of so exclusive a constitution as to render it of little
public benefit in the diffusion of knowledge
and learning. In fact it was, and to a large
extent is still, the luxurious literary lounge of
the wealthier classes of the colony, and its
shelves have contributed far more largely to
solace the intellectual leisure of busy men, than
to instruct, either by reading, or the publication of lucubrations arising from it, the Australian public. It is however a very valuable
institution, containing as it does a large number
of books of reference not to be found elsewhere, and to which any well-educated man,
for the purpose of reference, can easily find
access. On the recommendation of three
shareholders any person may now subscribe to
this library at the rate of three pounds per
annum, and such recommendation is easily
procurable by any well conducted and respectable man.

There is also an institution in Sydney, known
as the Mechanics' School of Arts, but a more
miserable misnomer for it could hardly be
conceived. Whatever may have been the design of its original founders, the last ten years
of its existence has certainly been objective to
no principle of good, while it has been
subjective to the admission of many
principles of evil. Its library, for the
most part, a miserable collection of

tattered novels; its museum, if its paltry collections deserve the name, an uncatalogued collection of unappreciable fossils, incomprehensible bones, and a few busts and medals, worthy the adornment of an itinerant dealer's stall; its lectures unconnected, and when delivered scarcely attended to, on subjects the most unfit for the instruction of an audience such as ought to attend such an institution; and from the mouths of men who were for the most part no authority on the themes on which they treated; brought into continual public contempt by the pitiable personalities which disfigure its management; the unseemly squabbles which under all changes seem to characterise its directory; and most of all by the same unswerving determination or fatuity which leads that directory to make a public institution, receiving public aid, effect the least possible amount of public good; the sooner this institution or mockery of an institution, which still "lives and languishes, and languishing doth live," gives up the ghost, the better for the literary prospects of the colony at large. It is painful, bitterly painful to have to make these observations of any literary institution in the colony; but they are the result of some watchful observation, uninfluenced by any connection, in any manner, at any time, with the society, during a long series of years.

Nor do we think we should do full justice to the complete and entire object of these papers, did we not exhibit fairly the state of such institutions as these. It is by no means degrading to the colony that this state of things should exist ; the institution was founded long years ago on principles in accordance with the spirit, or rather the prejudices of the age, and it worked out its object at first with tolerable success. But it is only since that period that those very principles have been exploded in England, and literary institutions, whether for the poor or the rich, for the educated or ignorant, for the student or the mechanic, for the theoretically artistic and scientific professor or the practically artistic and scientific artizan, have been established on a broader basis,—a foundation more consistent with the magnificent structure to be reared upon it ; possessing elements more effective for the instruction, and therefore more conducive to the happiness of the human race.

It is therefore with somewhat of subdued satisfaction that we look upon the approaching extinction of this institution, confident that upon its ashes will arise another literary and scientific society, worthy of the gigantic grasp which the cultivated intellect of the nineteenth century ought to take on any shore or in any sphere. An institution which shall unfold through its agencies to the thousands and the millions who will resort to this great continent, the boundless resources of its soil and climate ; which shall make the hidden tunnel of the miner, and the dark channel of the rushing stream, the easy path to boundless wealth. Which shall teach with classic taste the innate genius of the humble artizan to form the precious metal, or the transparent marble, into shapes and imaginative combinations, which, infusing the artist's intellect into the dull stone or duller ore, shall enhance its value ten-fold. Which shall give to the comprehension of the humble mechanic the fullest knowledge of the operations in which he has engaged, and enable him more skilfully and more successfully to conduct them; and which shall withal, doing all this, instructing, ennobling, and enriching all, comfort moreover, and wipe off with a soothing hand, which none dull to literary sympathies wot of, that " sweat of the face," in which every man must " eat bread."

In some of the country towns, Parramatta, and Brisbane, in the Moreton Bay district, similar societies to that we have just been describing have been recently originated, and we hope they will carefully avoid the shoals on which the elder institution has foundered. Let them carefully consider their future course, and a bright future is before them, and while they will form one of the brightest and best attractions to this wonderful land, they also will lend a most effective aid to the development of its productive and industrial resources.

There are several passive national scientific institutions in the colony, but they do not flourish, simply for the want of that interest in them which the more active societies for the cultivation of literature and science can alone inspire. We have a museum, which is capable of exhibiting an unlimited collection of curiosities, but it is the miserable policy of the Government and the legislature to cut off this institution from being instructive or even amusing. Rich in specimens, the treasures are laid up to corrupt and rust in chests, instead of being exhibited in the halls of the building, erected at a very considerable national expense. Its officer, for strange as it may sound, there is but one, unless he be a doorkeeper, is but miserably paid; although the industry and talent he has displayed entitle him to all praise, and it is evident a higher and better spirit must exist through the community before the full benefit of this institution can be made apparent.

The same remarks will hold good with regard to the Botanic Gardens of Sydney. Surpassing in natural picturesque beauty almost anything of the kind in the world, with an aspect and a capability by the adaptation of soils to the growth of almost every plant, any attempt to render them a really scientific institution, to confer benefit on the community, is nullified by the wretched parsimony with which they are treated by the legislature of the country. Casting out of all consideration the original objects of the gardens as conveyed in their title—"the preamble" we suppose to their act of incorporation for the public good, we do not remember one shilling to have been voted for the botanic enrichment of these gardens. The salaries of the director, the superintendent, and the wages of the labourers are reluctantly and grudgingly paid, and a debate ensues whether £40 shall be voted for the construction of a drain, or the erection of a fence, but a proposition to have a thousand pounds a year to properly classify the plants to send to foreign countries or neighbouring islands to fill up the intervals which occur in such classification, would be shuddered at and negatived by a convulsive shake of the head.

But until these things are properly remedied the colony of New South Wales will have no really useful Botanic Gardens. Beauitful as a lounge for the public they undoubtedly are; useful for the student in botany they are not, and consequently are comparatively useless as a means whereby the industrial enterprise of the colony may be assisted.

The only other literary institution which is worthy of mention, is the highest that exists, " the Press."

New South Wales is by no means deficient in her men of education, of reflection, of study and observation, nay, even of considerable depth of erudition.

She has had her historians, her explorers, her fiction writers, and her poets, but perhaps taking all things into consideration, the less said of the works of these literary artists the better ; not that they are by any means contemptible in themselves, but that as viewed in comparison with the writings of the authors of the old world, associated as they are with all the recollections of past pomp and pageantry, the rude history or poetic descriptions of a semi-barbarous land would attract but little attention. Twenty years hence, when New South Wales is growing into a great nation, we well believe she will possess in full proportion to her other attributes the power of literary and scientific eminence. It is written in the character of the people that what they want, they will have ; and in the better classes of society nothing is more longed for than literary and scientific distinction.

With regard to its newspaper press, New South Wales may fairly challenge competition with any colony in the world. It possesses at present two daily newspapers, which on the whole, with considerable ability and strict impartiality, review the leading topics of the day.

There are besides several weekly papers, but at the present moment they can scarcely be said to fulfil their vocation as collators of news, as they are devoted almost exclusively to party purposes. Numbers of successfully established newspapers have gone down in New South Wales, not for the want of a certain sort of erratic talent which marked their conduct, but from the absence of that steady business-like management which is essential to the stability of the periodical press.

We have now concluded those remarks which we thought it necessary to make in reference to certain topics not under the general scope of these papers. We might have taken in many other subjects, such as its Governmental Constitution, its jurisprudence, and its municipal regulations. We find, however, these would not only lead us too far a-field but would distract the attention of the reader from the original design of these papers,—the physical capabilities of the colony, under the influence of the industrial operations of man. We therefore abstain from further comment, and pause, ere we conclude, for a moment, to view calmly the position in which the colony of New South Wales at present stands.

First of all the colonies of Great Britain in the attention at present bestowed upon her— first in all the permanent and intrinsic advantages which can fit her to take the leading place among England's colonies ;—what are her pretensions, and what are her destinies?

To the former question we point to her thousands of cultivated acres rich with the crops of almost unskilled cultivation. To her boundless plains studded with millions of sheep and cattle—to her mines worked only with vigour and energy when ONE METAL, and that the most precious is found nearly on the surface—to her extending trade, her prodigious wealth, and more, far more than all, to what we believe to be the indomitable energies of the present inhabitants, for subduing the land and replenishing it.

To the latter we would answer that looking at all that has been done, from north to south and from east to west, there is still ample room and verge enough to multiply that doing a hundred times over ; rich in the possession of political rights she never held before, and which, if not all she is entitled to by birthright as a daughter of Britain, are good and sufficient security of her possessing her own in their fulness hereafter ; rich in material prosperity ; rich in the inexhaustible energies of a great, thriving, and enterprising population, demanding from her parent not that which that parent craves, but which it is but too willing to cast off, – its redundant labour ; the community of New South Wales may at this present period regard themselves in respect to their material prosperity, their social and moral security, as the most flourishing community on the face of the earth.

But in the contemplation of this material prosperity, this social and moral security, the future must be taken into consideration, and, even viewed by the most philosophic eye, this future must be regarded as more bright, more pregnant with greatness than the present. How magnificent the vista of future greatness through which the eye of Australian prophecy pierces !

A land under industrial enterprise, flowing with milk and honey ; rich with the vine, the

pomegranate, and the fig; with flocks and
herds, with teeming cities, with fertile plains
and mountains, whose ravines and streamlets
are but the index to inexhaustible wealth.
Upon the highest pinnacle of the mountain
citadels of this land the Australian seer might
stand, and surveying all before and below
him, exclaim in the language of Scripture,
"Behold! it is very good." He might from
his eminence, gifted with the eye of prescience,
behold the wild luxuriant plains, the
lofty hills, the torrent torn but dried up
water-courses, assuming before the giant step of
colonization the aspect and the form of civilised
society. He might too see with far foreseeing
eye, and hear with long expectant ear, the
triumphal train, and the rattling of the chariots
along the iron roads which will, ere many years
be past, intersect every district of this colony.
He might, too, unloosing his vision from the
almost boundless expanse of the material
world before him, cast forth his glance into the
dim mysteries of the coming time, and proclaim
that Australia must not only be a people, but
the "mother of many nations."

Girded round by resources absolutely unknown, and unappreciated by the older countries of the world at their origin, what destiny
is too high for her to fulfil? Every innate and
outward intelligence that inspire us—the re-
cords of history, the predictions of prophecy,
the aspirations of ambition, the deductions of
philosophy, the dictates of reason, and the

common instincts of our race, all alike proclaim that colonization is the divine mission of nations.

On these shores, the remotest from those we most reverentially remember, should we forget this truth ? Should we, the primest and the fairest offspring of that proud parent land, whose venerable smile beams with benignant dignity upon a world, forget the high vocation to which we are likewise called.

Shortly, very shortly, we shall be called on to exercise for ourselves the prerogative of self-government ; for in the history of " the nations as they pass away," centuries can only be reckoned as moments.

The oldest, the most regal daughter of Great Britain in the southern world, disciplined in affliction and humiliation in her earlier years, will not forget the heritage intrusted to her ; and when in the fulfilment of her time she shall wield the sceptre of her own dominion under the benign and approving eye of that venerable parent, let her not forget *her* mission ; may she remember in the immensity of her own regeneration how much may be done in the work of civilization, and let her not forget that to keep the Nations, children that she will yet beget, in degradation and subserviency, is but to renew the sackcloth and ashes, beneath which the springtide of her own youth has bowed.

Thankful amongst other blessings may New South Wales be, for that she is appointed as the apparent centre, the chief point, from which the colonization of the beautiful isles of the Pacific will spring ; carefully should she —once a stray waif in the world, but now the proudest scion of the British family—use her growing greatness to protect and keep these islands from lawless rapine until the day arrives when they will become especially her own. By example, by an arduous and steady cultivation of the arts of peace, in despite of some physical difficulties, in despite of her remoteness from the Western civilization ; few, none who reflect well and deeply, can doubt that the Australias are destined to become a great nation.

Let them become so in that genuinely progressive spirit, which, seeking only in its worldly politics to ameliorate and improve the condition of humanity, shall leave to the pure and simple Christianity which is the sole beautifier and perfector of all human institutions, that regeneration of our race which is promised and foretold.

NOTES.

Whaling Statistics, p. 115.—At the time this was written it was proposed to add a statistical appendix, but the idea was subsequently abandoned. The information will be found in the chapter on Commerce.

Minerals, p. 138.—Rock Salt and Emery, both existing in abundance, have been omitted here.

School of Arts, p. 270.—We are desirous that our remarks upon this institution should be understood as having reference to its whole course of management, and not, as some have interpreted them, to the present Directory. We admit that, for some time past, not only have strenuous efforts been made to render the institution really efficient, but that many improvements have been effected. But we are convinced that these exertions, praiseworthy as they are, can be productive of no tangible and permanent advantage unless the institution be wholly remodelled.

Check Out More Titles From HardPress Classics Series In this collection we are offering thousands of classic and hard to find books. This series spans a vast array of subjects – so you are bound to find something of interest to enjoy reading and learning about.

Subjects:
Architecture
Art
Biography & Autobiography
Body, Mind &Spirit
Children & Young Adult
Dramas
Education
Fiction
History
Language Arts & Disciplines
Law
Literary Collections
Music
Poetry
Psychology
Science
…and many more.

Visit us at www.hardpress.net